HIDDEN TREASURES

NORTH WEST LONDON VOL II

Edited by Rachael Radford

First published in Great Britain in 2002 by
YOUNG WRITERS
Remus House,
Coltsfoot Drive,
Peterborough, PE2 9JX
Telephone (01733) 890066

All Rights Reserved

Copyright Contributors 2002

HB ISBN 0 75433 822 3
SB ISBN 0 75433 823 1

Foreword

This year, the Young Writers' Hidden Treasures competition proudly presents a showcase of the best poetic talent from over 72,000 up-and-coming writers nationwide.

Young Writers was established in 1991 and we are still successful, even in today's technologically-led world, in promoting and encouraging the reading and writing of poetry.

The thought, effort, imagination and hard work put into each poem impressed us all, and once again, the task of selecting poems was a difficult one, but nevertheless, an enjoyable experience.

We hope you are as pleased as we are with the final selection and that you and your family continue to be entertained with *Hidden Treasures North West London Vol II* for many years to come.

Contents

Beis Yaacov (Beth Jacob) Primary School
    Esti Rosenfeld   1
    Esti Weisz   2

Blessed Dominic RC Primary School
    Thomas Donno   3
    Lacie Southon   3
    Matthew Thomas   4
    Christel J Gomez   4
    Catherine Carroll   5
    Shani   5
    Vicki Sneddon   5
    Dannielle Taylor   6
    Kareen Linton   6
    Sean Fox   7

Fairway Primary School
    Kenesha Henry   7
    Joanna Aponso-Ramirez   8
    Punam Shah   8
    Sruthi Gnanasubramanian   9
    Parsa Sadigh   10
    Imran Choudhury   10
    Alicia San José   10
    Rikki Bell   11
    Keely-Ann Dunning   11
    Roshnee Patel   12
    Shamil Solanki   12
    Roshan Patel   13
    Lauren Maley   13
    Amy Popplewell   13
    Daryl Glynn   14
    Florian Culka   15
    Ayesha Habib   15
    Radhika Raja   16
    Rahul Bahal   16

Nisha Shah	17
Samsam Mohamed	17
Sanketh Rampes	18
Raynor Dinham	18
Amir Amirani	19
Daiyaan Ghani	20
Vishaan Mohindra	20
Zara Hason	21
Matthew Dear	21
Lauren Roche	22
Patricia Curson	22
Meera Patel	23
Ramith Gunawardena	23
Alex Michael	24
Kayleigh Devine	24
Sumeet Brar	24
Jessica Cooper	25
Benjamin Ko	25
Hannah Brown	26
Sahil Kunder	26
Ekta Bahal	27
Jade Kelly	27
Kumbi Kuti	28
Neha Haria	28
Monica Depala	29
Heidi Ko	29
Mary-Kate Hickman	30
Jenna Sellars	30
Amanda Botros	31
Vimal Depala	32
Sarah Baxter	33
Olawale Odusoga	34
Hrishikesh Nimalraj	34
Amber Gifford	35

Islamia Primary School

Huda Abbas	35
Lyibah Ahmed	36

Abdulla Al-Diraa	36
Aaishah Ahmed	37
Maryum Khan	37
Saffat Shah	37
Hinna Mohammed	38
Tasleemah Pandore	38
Amir Shaw	38
Hiba Chaudhry	39
Safiyah Ali	39
Faizah Anisa-Kahn	40
Zobia Hussain	40
Muniza Aziz	40
Nashwa Ali	41
Kamilah Abdelrahim	41
Arqam Umar Ahmad	42
Yasmen Mir	42
Mehreen Hanslot	43
Zahida Ashraf	44
Asmaa Shah	44
Hala Bashir	44
F Nabilah El-Harraj	45
Mustafa Hamid	45
Zahrah Khan	46
Miriam Ahmed	47
Amir Aouf	47
Zain Raja	47
Yusuf Sherwani	48
Salima Boukhemia	49
Aneesa Habaik	49
Maryam Halaoui	50
Taahira Faruque	50
Husam Hamid	50
Marium Sherwani	51
Amirah Anwara Abdu'Allah	51
Noor Al Houda Elterk	52
Karima Segayer	52
Imad el-deen Halaoui	53
Aadil Ahmed	54

Muath Tawfiq	54
Shezaad A R Raja	55
Aisha Rashid	56
Siddeeqa Rashid	56
Gofran Sawalha	57
Mahmood Sharaf	57
Zainab Rashid	58
Shaymaa Sourroukh	58
Sarah Rhalem	59
Sumayya Ahmad	59
Zahra Mughal	59
Marwa Radwan	60
Yasmin Hasan	60
Maymuna Shaheem	61
Sarah Sourroukh	61
Ibah Ahmad	62

Lyndhurst House School

Daniel Attiyah	62
Alexander Allen	63
Toby Gould	63
William Barakat	64
Dominic Barnard	64
Isaac Epstein	65
Oliver Gafsen	66
Naoya Shimizu	66
Denis Konoplev	67
Aria Khani	67
Adam D Robinow	68
Joel Freedman	69
Adam Zwierzynski	70
David Khalastchi	70
Riccardo Lara	70
Sam Hardcastle	71
Shamil Dudhia	71
David Zargaran	72
Milton Karamani	72
Imran Basri	73

Kunal Choraria	73
Samuel Taylor	74
Yuki Oka	74
Justen Barget	75
Aryan Alipour	75
Ben Rabinovich	76
Chris Cronin	77
Mark Keisner	77
Adam Barget	78
David Keisner	78
Oliver Sharpstone	79
Kevin Tan	79
Nikola Govedarica	80

Mathilda Marks-Kennedy School

Bar Hariely	80
Nadav Albin	81
Amy Boekstein	81
Sophie Mattes	82
Natasha Pein	82
Adam Lewis	83
Jonathan Black	84
Elliot Zabaroff	84
Joshua Goodman	85
Nadav Ezra	85
Elana Freeman	86
Claudia Stone	86
Liron Mannie	87
Daniel Brovman	87
Gabriella Mannie	88
Jordan Ezekiel	88
Aden Amsellem	88
Ruby Moss	89
Rachel Barnberg	89
Yoav Greenberg	89
Danielle Michelson	90
Maya Solnitzky	90
Lauren Lightstone	91

Ben Goldberg	91
Zoe Ilivitzky	92
Tomm Shkoury	92
Talya Robinson	93
Noga Livne	93
Michael Obadia	94
Harriet Strauss	94
Jonathan Artman	95
Gaby Levey	95
Rishana Hikmet	96
Louis Grant	96
Gavin Fox	97
Libby Morris	97
Shir Shafran	98
Daniel Lester	98
Gil Albin	99
Laura Nouriel	99
Natasha Berg	100
Tamir Chitiyat	100
Moty Shemtov	101
Michael Kosky	101
Nicola Boekstein	102
Jake Mimoni	103
Alisa Sacofsky	104
Robert Lewis	104
Jacob Hilton	105
Deborah Elf	106
Adam Mimoni	106
Joshua Jacobs	107
Gemma Ashken	107
Nathan Pomerance	108
Gideon Caplin	108
Rachel Schraer	109
Yael Shafritz	110
Shira Mass	110
Marcus Freeman	111
Ronelle Lang	112
Daniel Cohen	113

Roe Green Junior School
- Pooja Varsani — 113
- Sarah Pirbhai — 114
- Aroshana Haththotuwa — 114
- Charlote Aguallo — 115
- Jaina Patel — 115
- Sinthuja Subashkaran — 116
- Nikhil Savani — 117
- Matthew Brown — 117
- Sivasankar Sivakumar — 118
- Pritesh Patel — 118
- Mohamed Tamam — 119
- Priya Rabadia — 119
- Miten Thakrani — 120
- Muneba Iqbal — 120
- Reema Patel — 121
- Myuran Ranganathan — 121
- Seanie Joseph — 122
- Panitaj Bhudia — 122
- Rozina Sabur — 123
- Shakti Shah — 123
- Komal Patel — 124
- Hasani James — 124
- Preena Popat — 124
- Anand Joshi — 125
- Zahra Khan — 125
- Kiran Manji — 126
- Rhys Mulikita — 126
- Shazia Kassam — 127
- Bunsri Bhuwa — 127
- Shireen Mohammad — 128
- Jahni Thomas — 128
- Nidhi Shah — 128
- Sandeep Bharj — 129
- Ramindra Pal M Darma Pal — 129
- Melissa Calleja — 129

The Poems

SCHOOL

I run into school, help I'm late,
My hair's all messy, I'm in a terrible state.
I sit down, the teacher's all red,
She obviously got out the wrong side of the bed.

I take out my books really fast,
She always shouts 'cause I'm last.

The subject of history that is first,
Typical, that would be my worst.

Break I look forward to eagerly,
'Who's going to play jump rope with me?'

After this it's maths 'Oh no,'
But it's better than English to which we must go.
4+4 she's pointing to me,
I don't know it, can't she see.

Lunch is now, it's when we can eat,
I hope Mum packed me a real nice treat.

Next we have lessons and lessons more,
And get packed with homework galore.

But one thing I always look forward to,
Is the bell, which rings at 4.32.

Children wildly jump out the gate,
And get really frantic when their mum comes late
And then from school home we'll run
After a tired day we need some fun.

Esti Rosenfeld
Beis Yaacov (Beth Jacob) Primary School

THE WINTER STAGES

The trees are hesitating to let their leaves fall down
And sweep along the edge of the cracked pavement
The wind begins to blow and blow until it manages
To penetrate throughout.

Suddenly flashes of lightning streak across the sky.
The sound of rolling thunder echoes in the streets;
Swish swosh, the wind blows calmly and then . . .
Thunder, lightning strikes again.
Magnificent colours appear in the sky and perform
A dazzling rainbow.

A small smile appears on the lips of the people,
Here come along the hailstones that prick against our backs
And tears of happiness, joyfulness as we discover
The gentle snowflakes.

Time to put on boots, coats etc, time to go outside,
Something to watch.

The snow starts falling, the slippery mixture of ice and water
Combining together.
Time to dress warmly.

Our legs become stiff and our fingers are numb with cold,
The wind gives a strong breeze.
Now it is perfectly clear . . .

Winter has arrived! Enjoy!

Esti Weisz (10)
Beis Yaacov (Beth Jacob) Primary School

ARSENAL FC

Arsenal is my best team
I watch their matches all the time.
They have dazzling skills,
With fantastic goals.

We have players from around the globe,
Who put on a spectacular show.
People call Arsenal boring,
It's just that they get all the glory.

Arsenal are just the best,
Better than all the rest.
When we play Man United or Liverpool,
We always come out the winners of all.

Thomas Donno
Blessed Dominic RC Primary School

MY FAVOURITE TV SHOW

I've got a favourite TV show
And until it's over no one should try and move me.
From summer in the sun to winter with the snow,
I can't even have a snack in case I miss a bit to do a wee.
There's only three left,
So it's getting very tense.
I hope I've given you a clue to the programme you will guess.
It takes a lot of commitment but no expense.
There is talent of the best
As the pressure piles up
I'll tell you who it is before you go to rest.

Lacie Southon
Blessed Dominic RC Primary School

THE MAN WHO LIVES ON SILENT HILL

The man who lives on Silent Hill
Comes out at night and wants to kill.
When he spots you wander by
He will let out an almighty cry
And curse your body till you die.

The man who lives on Silent Hill
Sits motionless at his windowsill,
When suddenly the sky turns black
And his whole pale body starts to crack,
His hands crinkle and his eyes turn red,
And all of a sudden . . . he's *dead.*

Matthew Thomas
Blessed Dominic RC Primary School

KING OF THE JUNGLE

In the jungle far away,
Animals, wild cats cry today.
High great swingers, tree to tree,
No more taller than my knee.
Hear the sound of beating wings,
And sweet feelings as it sings.
A mad reptile starts to hiss,
To catch its prey, it doesn't miss.
Furthermore a scary sound,
His black chest he begins to pound.
Stop! Here comes a triumph yell,
King of the jungle, I can tell.

Christel J Gomez
Blessed Dominic RC Primary School

THE BEST AUNTY IN THE WORLD

My aunty Lena is so nice
She makes food with a spice,
She lives in a town called Yate
For an aunty she's my best mate.

Her hair is short and brown
She's always smiling, never a frown
She likes my hair when it's curled
She's the best aunty in the world.

Catherine Carroll
Blessed Dominic RC Primary School

UNTITLED

My name is Shani
I can be very lazy.

My best friend Matty
Could be very chatty.

My friend Cynthia
Likes telling jokes and makes me laugh
Until I choke.

Shani
Blessed Dominic RC Primary School

MY SISTER

My sister is annoying who is always chasing boys.
Listening to garage music, what a noise.
She is kind and loveable when she is not stressed.
That is my sister Denise.

Vicki Sneddon
Blessed Dominic RC Primary School

Jungle Life

Quietly the snapper's snapping
Then he hears a quiet tapping

Then he hears a silent creeping
Whilst the animals lie sleeping

The human disturbs the snapper's house
While snapper is as quiet as a mouse

Snapper lies in the shade
Waiting for dinner to be made

He's waiting, waiting for dinner
'Cause the human is a sinner

Snap! Snap! Goes snapper's mouth
Then silently the life pours our.

Dannielle Taylor
Blessed Dominic RC Primary School

The Waterfall

The waterfall thundered
Sending splashes into the air.
Sparkling droplets sprinkled everywhere
Cascading over the rocks below
Heading into the big blue sea.
Flying fishes are jumping through the air
While small thin fishes swim
Everywhere!

Kareen Linton
Blessed Dominic RC Primary School

AUTUMN

The days are darker and colder,
The weather is rough and wet,
The year is getting older,
So turn up the heat my pet.

The wind and rain are wild,
The leaves are starting to fade,
The weather is no longer mild,
But soon new trees will be made.

The snow will start to melt,
The leaves will stop being piled,
People will no longer pelt,
You and your small little child.

Sean Fox
Blessed Dominic RC Primary School

COLOURS

Yellow yellow you taste like marshmallows.
Blue blue are you new?
Green green why are you so mean?
White white please don't bite.
Purple purple can I touch your turtle?
Black black have you changed your name to Mack?
Pink pink you make the boys wink.
Red red get in your bed.
Brown brown don't let me down.
Gold gold you have grown old.

Kenesha Henry (9)
Fairway Primary School

IN THE GARDEN

In the garden as you can see, there is a big tree,
As you can see it's only for me.

In the garden as you can see, the grass is made of brass,
It's also just for me.

In the garden as you can see, there is a swing just for me,
And every day I have to sing.

In the garden as you can see, there is a slide just for me,
And every day I hide behind the slide.

In the garden as you can see, look up in the sky,
See clouds fly by, in them you can see a creature,
But it's really my teacher.

Joanna Aponso-Ramirez (9)
Fairway Primary School

RAIN

It comes every day,
I can't go out to play.

I have to sit inside the boring house,
And watch our cat eat the mouse.

I can't have picnics or go to the park,
But instead I have to hear the dog bark.

I hate these days they bore me to death,
So now I have decided to stay in bed.

I hate rain!

Punam Shah (9)
Fairway Primary School

WEATHER

January brings the snow
Cars go very slow

February brings the sleet
Tickling your hands and feet

March brings gales, very shrill
Whistling round the daffodils

April showers fall soft and slow
Earth wakes up and green things grow

May brings leaves on trees
And flowers for the buzzing bees

June brings lots of garden showers
That help to water all the flowers

July brings the holidays
Forget about your boring days

August brings the fun and sunshine
Every day the weather's fine

September brings the cold and breeze
Making all our faces freeze

October brings the freezing chill
I thought that is really brill

November brings the freezing cold
Making leaves turn into gold

December brings the fastest snow
Making all our faces glow.

Sruthi Gnanasubramanian (8)
Fairway Primary School

AGE

When I was one I twisted my tongue.
When I was two I was too cool.
When I was three I had a degree.
When I was four I was poor.
When I was five I had a beehive.
When I was six I had my first Twix.
When I was seven I looked up at Heaven.
When I was eight I had a debate.
Now that I am nine I am fine.

Parsa Sadigh (9)
Fairway Primary School

DOWN IN THE GOAL AREA

Down in the goal area
I met a player called Owen
Owen said 'I can't play now
I'm going to make a poem
Down in the goal area
I met a player called Zola
Zola said 'I can't play now
Because I need to drink some cola.'

Imran Choudhury (8)
Fairway Primary School

DOWN IN THE PLAYGROUND

Down in the playground
I met a boy called Nick
Nick said 'I can't play now
I am going home to pick.'

Down in the playground
I met a girl called Rose
Rose said 'I can't play now
I've got a sniffy nose.'

Alicia San José (8)
Fairway Primary School

MY FRIEND CALLED ED

There was Ed who was dead
He was dead lying on his bed
His mate called Fred who said
My friend was dead
Because he jumped and landed on his head
When he was going to bed
Before Ed was dead he said
'I have a good head
That's why I'm going to be dead'
So Ned said 'Don't land on your head'
And that was the story of a man called Ed.

Rikki Bell (10)
Fairway Primary School

STARLIGHT

Starlight star bright
In the middle of the night.
See it twinkle really bright,
Starlight star bright.
When you are in the stars
It looks like you're looking at mars.
Starlight star bright.

Keely-Ann Dunning (8)
Fairway Primary School

TWENTY BROKEN BOOKS

Twenty broken books
Nineteen messy cooks
Eighteen silly hats
Seventeen colourful mats
Sixteen jumpy frogs
Fifteen hidden logs
Fourteen grizzly bears
Thirteen tiny pears
Twelve dirty cars
Eleven bright stars
Ten alarm clocks
Nine metal rocks
Eight golden bats
Seven ugly rats
Six small drops
Five growing crops
Four bottles of creams
Three different ice creams
Two iced cakes
One slithering snake.

Roshnee Patel (9)
Fairway Primary School

UNTITLED

Down on the hill
I met a boy called Bow
Who said 'I can't play now
I'm going home to sow.'

Shamil Solanki (7)
Fairway Primary School

THE WEATHER HERE AND THERE

Isn't it funny
How India is sunny
While in London it's cold
At least that's what I've been told
Over there it's light
And the sky is bright
But here it is raining
Without any warning
I could have a lovely day
So rain get out of my way.

Roshan Patel (10)
Fairway Primary School

DOWN IN THE SHOE SHOP

Down in the shoe shop
I met a girl called Jo
Jo said 'I've got to go'
She ran out of the door
And left her shoe on the floor.

Lauren Maley (7)
Fairway Primary School

DOWN IN THE LANE

Down in the lane
I met a Great Dane
I left him there
I had a pear
And then I said it was fair.

Amy Popplewell (8)
Fairway Primary School

SCHOOL

I'm a pupil at Fairway School,
I think it's really cool!
I am in my last year
And I live really near.

My teacher is Mrs Young,
She likes songs to be sung.
Miss Kidner is really fun,
Forget the homework I'm on the run.

My favourite sport is football,
My worst sport is netball.
I play football for the school,
I hate it when it is four all.

Maths is the best,
Forget about the rest.
My handwriting is quite neat,
Because I sit still on my seat.

My friends are all kind,
Which is really nice to find.
We have had moments when we have laughed,
Because most of us are daft.

Seven years have gone fast,
Especially the last.
Soon I have to move on
And then I will be gone.

Daryl Glynn (10)
Fairway Primary School

THE BIG BLACK

I wonder what's in the black,
If I could touch it with my hand,
Or go there in a spaceship
To discover any land.

I want to find aliens
Like they show on the TV,
I wonder if they can speak
Or if they just say 'Bee bee.'

I want to see Saturn's rings,
And see if Mercury's hot,
I don't mind seeing just Mars,
But I'd like to see the lot!

Even if I like the black,
There is still a place I long,
For this place is on the Earth,
My home is where I belong!

Florian Culka (11)
Fairway Primary School

WHEN I WENT . . .

When I went to school I landed in a pool
Then the teacher said
'Are you dead?'

When I went home
I picked up the phone to phone my friend
And I said 'Don't call me now, I'm going up to bed.'

Ayesha Habib (7)
Fairway Primary School

WHEN I SAW IT

When I saw it
It was yellow
And was in a pit.
It was picking on marshmallows.

The hairy thing
Was a little bee.
It had a broken wing.
The bee was looking at my tea.

It bit me,
The little rat,
In the middle of the sea,
Just like a bat.

Radhika Raja (10)
Fairway Primary School

THE MONSTER IN THE DOOR

The monster in the door
Lives on the fifth floor.
He has one eye
And isn't shy.
He's always jumping around
But doesn't make a sound.
His name is James
And he likes to play games.
His friend's name is Boo
And he always gives her goo.
That's the monster in the door
Would you like to hear more?

Rahul Bahal (10)
Fairway Primary School

THE RAT

A little boy, five in May
Got a pet rat
Her name was Lucy
She was black and grey.

Playing in the garden, two days ago
Lucy went missing
Did some rat trapper take her away
Went down to the RSPCA.

Told me not to worry
It would be just fine
Nothing more to do
Just hope and pray.

Nisha Shah (11)
Fairway Primary School

WEATHER

January new beginning
Resolutions, snowflakes spinning
February frosty fogs
Winter shivers, fire, warm logs
March blows windy, smells of spring
Leaves peek out, brave blackbirds sing
April showers fall soft and slow
Earth wakes up and green things grow
May day ribbons round a pole
May time babies lambs and foals
June brings summer blasting in
Scent roses sun on skin.

Samsam Mohamed (7)
Fairway Primary School

TEN WHITE SNOWMEN

Ten white snowmen feeling just fine
One fell over then there were nine.

Nine white snowmen standing on a plate
One hit himself then there were eight.

Eight white snowmen looking at Devon
One got tired then there were seven.

Seven white snowmen eating Weeatbix
One didn't feel well then there were six.

Six white snowmen playing near a hive
One got stung by a bee then there were five.

Five white snowmen watching some more
One burnt his leg then there were four.

Four white snowmen playing with a bee
One got stung then there were three.

Three white snowmen saying 'Moo'
One got a sore throat then there were two.

Two white snowmen having fun
One didn't have fun then there was one.

One white snowman having a son
He had a heart attack then there were none.

Sanketh Rampes (7)
Fairway Primary School

UNTITLED

Gliding as he comes off the ground
Like a piece of paper being thrown into the sky.
Flying higher and higher still
Like a person climbing up the stairs.

Fluttering backwards as he sees the storm
Like humans running away from their troubles.
Swirling round and round as he's caught in the storm
Like a toilet being flushed.

Raynor Dinham (9)
Fairway Primary School

LADY IN RED

It was 8.00,
I got to the place I always meet her, she wasn't there yet.
I was worried.
I thought to myself, is it possible that I'm late
And she was gone?

It was 8.10 now -
The weather was cold, where was she?
I was looking at the direction she always came from.

It was 8.30 now,
Little by little I got stressed.
I said to myself, where on earth is she?
It was at 8.45 that I saw a misty shadow of her.
Oh, yes it was her!
She was coming closer to me with her red frock.
She was very attractive.
When I saw her all my anger went away.
Now, I couldn't believe my eyes, yes!
It was here - the 186 bus
Going to Edgware, it was here!

Amir Amirani (11)
Fairway Primary School

CELEBRITY MIX UP

I was looking for treasure when I found,
Before my eyes hidden surprises,
Was it a dog running away,
Or was it someone watching Home and Away?
Was it Homer Simpson drinking beer,
Or was it Gary Lineker pulling his ear?
Was it a teacher with a bad cough,
Or was it Britney Spears screaming her head off?
Was it a stranger making weird glances,
Or was it Harry Potter with broken glasses?
Was it a baby, a face of happiness,
Or was it Simon Cowell with everyday angriness?
Was it the music in Stars in Your Eyes,
Or was it Cilla Black saying 'Surprise surprise'?
Was it the hunters trapping parrots,
Or was it Bugs Bunny eating carrots?
Was it Chris Tarrant the millionaire,
Or was it Robbie Williams showing his underwear?
All these treasures I thought I would find,
Within the pages of my TV guide.

Daiyaan Ghani (10)
Fairway Primary School

THERE WAS A BOY CALLED VISHAAN

There was a boy called Vishaan
Who went to visit a barn
He saw a hen and drew it with a pen
So the hen moved and he said 'Oh darn!'

Vishaan Mohindra (11)
Fairway Primary School

THE BEAUTIFUL LAKE

The plants and grass are green, the lake is relaxing blue,
The sensational sun makes my soul relaxed from head to shoe.
The ducks are squealing and screaming their pitches high,
And now I can see they are one metre high.
'Oh look Davie there goes a boat with super speed'
The wind gone by the boat scattered the seeds.
The horizon of the two shades of blue meet,
The lake is just now touching my feet.
The birds are swooping,
Soaring high and looping.
Some families are having a picnic,
With scrumptious lollies to lick.
Youngsters are racing down the park with their skates,
Having a great time with their mates.
Pensioners sitting on the bench resting,
While the birds are nesting.
Ripples are being made by young children in the lake,
And when it hits the duck they give a little shake.
I am going to go for a walk round the bend,
My poem has now come to an end.

Zara Hason (10)
Fairway Primary School

SCHOOL

September starts a fresh school year
New pupils feel a twinge of fear
Our Harvest festival's displayed
Our thanks to farmers duly made.

Matthew Dear (10)
Fairway Primary School

SEASON GREETINGS

Spring

Lambs are born blossom appears.
Now the summer's almost here.

Summer

The scent of roses appear all around
They appear mostly from under the ground.

Autumn

The leaves are falling the rain is pouring.
Time to go back, it's so boring!

Winter

It's frosty it's cold,
But Santa will be coming soon.
That's what I was told.

Lauren Roche (9)
Fairway Primary School

PATRICIA

P   is for panda as they roll in the grass,
A   is for apples that are on the trees,
T   is for tigers as they hunt their prey,
R   is for rabbits as they hop on the ground,
I   is for ink that I write with in my books,
C   is for cats when they purr when they are happy,
I   is for indoor games that we play at school,
A   is for anteater that sucks up the ants.

Patricia Curson (10)
Fairway Primary School

TV (TELEVISION)

My TV
Means everything to me!
Without it I would cry, scream and wail,
All I would do all day is listen to the wind and hail!
If my TV was taken away from me,
Curly curls standing on ends is what you'll see!
I hate not being able to watch it,
I tell my mum without it I'd be unfit!

You're reading this thinking:
This girl must be so lazy,
She must be utterly crazy!

But you should think to yourself:
Could I go without my wonderful TV?
'Cause I'm telling you, you couldn't, not even me!

Meera Patel (11)
Fairway Primary School

THE FAIRWAY

Fairway is great.
Its playground is enjoyable.
Its lessons are educational.
The assemblies are funny.
The school council improve the school a lot.
Miss Holms, Mrs Young, Mr Bacari and Mr Smith
Are very forceful teachers.
Mr Maynard is very enthusiastic
And Ms Parker is very energetic
Because of this Fairway children
Are eager to come to school.

Ramith Gunawardena (8)
Fairway Primary School

A Wednesday Horror

On Wednesday I go swimming with Mary
I hate it because she is so scary.
She has no teeth so if she smiles
I'd rather swim and swim for miles.
Smile back I would never,
I would go and leave forever.
Every time I wish to leave,
But when I do I feel relieved.
Go under water that's the only way,
To black out what she has to say.
Today we might have a new teacher.
Oh no! she's back that horrible creature.

Alex Michael (9)
Fairway Primary School

Food, Food, Food

Jelly, jelly, jelly, nice for your belly
Rice, rice, rice, not very nice
Ham, ham, ham, better than jam
Meat, meat, meat, really neat.

Kayleigh Devine (10)
Fairway Primary School

Spider

I have eight long legs,
And my body is soft,
And my food is great.

Sumeet Brar (10)
Fairway Primary School

FRIENDS

I have quite a lot of friends,
Who I play with each day,
And the time I hate the most,
Is when they are away.

I haven't got a best friend,
In fact, I've quite a few,
And if I were to choose one,
It's something I can't do.

And after Friday's over,
To miss them is a pain,
But when the weekend's over,
I see them all again.

I think that friends are kind,
And help me when I'm down,
They come along and help me,
To get a smile from a frown.

Jessica Cooper (9)
Fairway Primary School

MY CLASS

I had a beautiful class
Which always played with glass
They always cut their hand
Then covered it with sand
And now they play with grass.

Benjamin Ko (10)
Fairway Primary School

FUNNY FOODS

Breakfast time is fun for me
Because I get a cup of tea,
After that I have some cereal
And that fills me up till 12.15.

School lunches are nasty
Full with broccoli and parsley,
But I like the pud
It's tasty and sweet,
But ice cream is my favourite treat.

After school I get it all
Crisps, chocolate and cakes.
My mum tells me not to eat too much
As I'll get a belly ache.
Later comes my evening meal
Often I finish and feel ill.

Hannah Brown (8)
Fairway Primary School

AGES

When I was one I was fun
When I was two I had the flu
When I was three I broke my knee
When I was four I slammed a door
When I was five I had a sty
When I was six I learnt to mix
When I was seven I went to Devon
When I was eight I had a great mate
Now I am nine I'm just fine.

Sahil Kunder (8)
Fairway Primary School

ANIMALS

Small tall every size, what can they be?
The slithering shine, the big white tusks.

The different shapes, the small grey tail,
The fine swimmers.

The colourful looks, the brown jumper,
The two-legged walker, what can they be?
Snakes,
Elephants,
Mice,
Fishes,
Kangaroos,
Humans,
Animals!

Ekta Bahal (8)
Fairway Primary School

THE SUPPLY TEACHER WITH THE CANE

There once was a supply teacher,
I can't remember his name.
I do remember he had a big cane,
When he hit you with the cane
You would suffer severe pain.

Luckily it was only for a day,
That's what we thought anyway.
Week after week he would come back,
To scare us into learning,
I must say we all behaved and learnt.

Jade Kelly (10)
Fairway Primary School

WHAT MY BROTHER IS SCARED OF

My brother is scared of the dark because he can't see.
He's scared of the light because he sees his shadow
And he thinks it's a monster.
He's scared of a roar because he thinks it is a real lion roaring.
He's scared of cartoon characters because he thinks
They are going to pop out and chase him.
He's scared of when the music gets scarier and scarier
Because he thinks scary things are coming out.
He's scared of animals because he thinks they are going to chase him.
What is my brother not scared of?
Maybe his mum and dad, uncles and aunties and his sisters.
Scaredy cat! Scaredy cat! Sitting on the door mat.

Kumbi Kuti (8)
Fairway Primary School

THE GIANT

In the tall, dark castle where nobody has been,
There is a huge, grumpy giant who is very mean.
He sits in his chair waiting for food,
If he doesn't get any, he'll be in a bad mood.
His face is always unhappy, there's never a grin,
He searches for food, even in a bin.
His favourite meal is a girl and a boy,
He likes to devour it, when his mind is full of joy.
When you try to escape, he can see,
I hope he doesn't have you for his tea!
So, if you ever sneak in, always make sure
He never hears you, or he'll let out a roar.

Neha Haria (10)
Fairway Primary School

My Planet Blunt

On my planet Blunt everything is back to front,
It's a very strange place to be,
The cats bow-wow,
The dogs miaow,
And the goldfish lives in the tree,

The sky of green is a wonderful scene,
Set against the fields of blue,
A beautiful brown sun shines down,
From midnight to half past two,

And don't forget your etiquette,
If a Bluntian you should meet,
You say hello,
When about to go,
And shake goodbye with your feet!

Monica Depala (11)
Fairway Primary School

Storm

On a stormy Monday,
Boats going in and out,
Buildings falling down,
People running about.

Houses crashing to the ground,
Cars are flying all over the place
People are scampering around,
And people pulling funny faces.

Heidi Ko (9)
Fairway Primary School

STICKS AND STONES

Down at the bottom of my garden
I found some sticks and stones.
The sticks were brown and the stones were black.
So I put them in my basket.
I went to the house to ask my mum what I should do with them.
She said 'Make a band with your sticks and stones,'
But I didn't want to do that.
I went to my dad with my sticks and stones
And said 'What shall I do with my sticks and stones?'
He had a look and said 'Make a house with your sticks and stones.'
But I thought, how?
I went to my brother with my sticks and stones.
He said 'Make a gun a big, big gun.'
I said 'No.'
So I went outside, put them back and went into my room.

Mary-Kate Hickman (8)
Fairway Primary School

MY GUINEA PIG

I love my guinea pig,
He's cute, furry and white.
He does tricks for little old me
And he always gets them right.
He's got beady little eyes
And cute furry ears.
He's got big sharp, white teeth
And he grins and stares.

Jenna Sellars (11)
Fairway Primary School

THE NONSENSE GIRAFFE

The nonsense giraffe is so silly,
He acts like a silly Billy.
He has a long neck,
And likes to peck!

The nonsense giraffe is quite big,
And is as thin as a twig.
It's tall like my friend Paul
And always likes to crawl!

The nonsense giraffe is red,
He even goes to sleep in my bed!
He's obviously too tall to sleep in it,
And makes so much mess it looks like a pit!

The nonsense giraffe is always eating fish,
And when it's dinner time he never eats what's on his dish,
He likes to smell other animals' mess,
And goes to a party wearing any old silly dress!

The nonsense giraffe is as clear as glass,
That when he has ideas he never gives them in class.
He shops in Wall-Marts,
And is crazy about darts!

The nonsense giraffe is as strong as an ox,
And when it's cold he gets the chicken pox!
He's so tall you can't even measure him,
So now you se how silly he is just like a pin!

Amanda Botros (11)
Fairway Primary School

THE SEASONS

The winds are blowing like birds' wings
The winds are blowing like birds' wings
The storms are coming like evil cats
The storms are coming like evil cats
The snow is coming down like gentle snow
The snow is coming down like gentle snow
The leaves are coming down like rattlesnakes
The leaves are coming down like rattlesnakes
The waters are coming down like stones
The waters are coming down like stones
The blossoms are coming down like feathers
The blossoms are coming down like feathers
The breeze is blowing like the seas
The breeze is blowing like the seas
The clouds are swishing like cotton wool
The clouds are swishing like cotton wool
The swings are swinging like rocking chairs
The swings are swinging like rocking chairs
The sun is melting down the Earth
The sun is melting down the Earth
The grass is dancing with the wind
The grass is dancing with the wind
The petals are soft as babies' skin
The petals are soft as babies' skin
The heatwaves are raging like fire
The heatwaves are raging like fire
The sand is coming up like a sand storm
The sand is coming up like a sand storm
The trees are as green as apples
The trees are as green as apples.

Vimal Depala (8)
Fairway Primary School

FRIENDS

Friends are always there
Especially when you need them.
They make you laugh when you're down
They're always there to play
Especially in hot days!
They stick up for you when bullies come
Along and never leave you on your own
You always have more than one friend
When one friend's gone.
People always say you have a best friend
But really all your friends
Are your best friends.
Sometimes you fight with friends
But in the end you always will make up,
If you are true friends
True friends are best to me.
There are some friends that don't talk
Behind your back and never leave you
To deal with some things on your own
Like family problems!
Best friends are not important
All your best friends are like my friends
I think I have a lot
We always see each other at weekends
And that's what friends are for
This is about my friends (especially Jess Cox).

Sarah Baxter (9)
Fairway Primary School

RAIN, RAIN

Rain, rain gives me the pains
Rain, rain can never delay
Rain, rain all around the world
Makes so much flood everywhere
Even in Poland.
Road closed, town is empty
Schools are out
So people stay at home
And eat all the food.
Rain rain rainy day
Is the best day ever
Because there's no more school.

Olawale Odusoga (9)
Fairway Primary School

BALLS

If a football hits your head
You will feel a little weird;
If a rugby ball hits your head
You will feel a little dizzy;
If a bouncy ball hits your head
It will hurt a little bit;
But if a tennis ball hits your head
You will shake a little bit;
If a baseball hits your head
You will end up in bed
But if a cricket ball his your head
You will end up dead!

Hrishikesh Nimalraj (9)
Fairway Primary School

IF ONLY

If only we can be
Loving and caring.
If only you were there
When needed.
If only we succeed in happiness
And not sadness.
If only we can come together
And try to help each other.

If only we could have peace within the world
Within us, within you.

If only, if only!

Amber Gifford (9)
Fairway Primary School

THE THIEF

The thief, the thief,
Stole my gold,
Without permission,
Without being told.

The thief, the thief,
Creeps around at night,
And when you meet him,
He gives you a fright.

The thief, the thief,
Is put away,
And learns his lesson,
That crime doesn't pay.

Huda Abbas (9)
Islamia Primary School

WHO ARE FRIENDS?

Who are friends?
I don't know.
Please tell me, I want to know.
Are they nice? Are they kind?
Please tell me, I want to know.
Are they big? Are they small?
Please tell me, I want to know.
Are they hairy? Are they bald?
Please tell me, I want to know.
Are they fat? Are they skinny?
Please tell me, I want to know.
Please for goodness sake, I want to know!
If you don't tell me, I won't know.

Lyibah Ahmed (8)
Islamia Primary School

THE ROCKET

There once was a rocket
Which took more electricity than a socket
The rocket was in Mars
Which took off in barns
The rocket went into the air
But ended up crashing in a big big fair
It was broken at the top
And ended up getting fixed with a mop
It was time for the rocket to go to Earth
But it had one more place to go which was Perth
It got to Perth which was really hot
But sadly it got shot.

Abdulla Al-Diraa (10)
Islamia Primary School

War

A world full of sadness,
A world full of pain,
Children die needlessly,
Mothers cry in silence,
That's what I see on TV,
Look closely what do you see?
But one thing I wish for is a world full of peace.

Aaishah Ahmed (8)
Islamia Primary School

Sadness

Sadness is dark and grey,
It smells like a cut soft apple,
Sadness tastes like sour lemon,
It sounds like tapping water,
It feels like a lump in the neck,
Sadness lives in your tears.

Maryum Khan (9)
Islamia Primary School

Misery

Misery is dull and grey,
It smells like sharp thunder,
It tastes like salty tears,
It sounds like people crying,
It feels hard and bitter,
It lives in your sad eyes.

Saffat Shah (9)
Islamia Primary School

TRUE LIFE

There was a little boy
His eyes were rather droopy
Because of this the kids named him Snoopy.
Thinking through is mind
What will he do in life?
Where will he end up?
One thing for sure
By the grace of Allah
From strength to strength he shall go.

Hinna Mohammed (8)
Islamia Primary School

THE OLD MAN OF GREECE

There was an old man from Greece,
Who travelled from west to east,
He fell in a hole with a beast,
They had a big feast,
They ate in a park,
Out in the dark,
With a dog named Lark,
Who always wanted to bark.

Tasleemah Pandore (11)
Islamia Primary School

MY BABY PUPPY

My baby puppy is so lovely and furry.
My baby puppy is so lovely and soft.
My baby puppy is nice and cosy.
My baby puppy is lovely and clean.
My baby puppy is so shiny.

My baby puppy likes to eat a lot for him to grow.
My baby puppy is so sweet.
My baby puppy is as soft as a pebble
And I like to play with him.

Amir Shaw (8)
Islamia Primary School

FRIENDSHIP

Friendship is a hidden treasure,
That his hidden in my heart.
I have many friends hidden in my heart,
But no one knows who they are,
Just me and my friend know all our secrets,
That we don't want anybody else to know.
We care and love and play with each other.
I like my friends and they like me.
Me and my friends will always stay together
Because friendship never slips away.
Friendship is a hidden treasure
That is hidden in my heart.

Hiba Chaudhry (8)
Islamia Primary School

PIRATE POEM

A pirate was on the beach,
He was looking for a treasure,
He had a fat chest that ripped his vest,
When the pirate was looking for the treasure,
'Suddenly' when a beast appeared everyone disappeared.

Safiyah Ali (8)
Islamia Primary School

UP IN THE ATTIC AND DOWN IN THE CELLAR

In the moonlight in the dark,
Mouldy old suitcase,

Dumped right in the corner,
Gritty, crumbly, chalky baby clothes,

Rusty old clock with a bird
Sticking out,

Old mildewy wedding dress,
The stairs go creek up in the attic.

Faizah Anisa-Kahn (10)
Islamia Primary School

CLEANLINESS

I like to stay clean
I don't like to be mean

Clean clothes mean freshness
Cleanliness is happiness

Cleanliness is next to godliness
Clean thoughts lead to success

When the heart is clean
The world is a better place to be in.

Zobia Hussain (10)
Islamia Primary School

FRIENDSHIP

It's not just what you have done for me,
　That makes me love you so,
It's all the goodness of who you are,
　The friend I have come to know.

Whether we're near or far,
  Or seas apart,
Our friendship will remain,
  Until the end of time,
Friends are friends forever.

Muniza Aziz (10)
Islamia Primary School

WINTER POEM

Winter, winter is here,
Snow, snow is coming near,
Playing in the snow is really fun,
But it's freezing so I wish I were in the sun,
When you have a cold you feel very old,
Winter days are short and very cold,
We have to wrap up
And stay warm.
Winter days bring happiness
As Eid will be here soon.

Nashwa Ali (8)
Islamia Primary School

FLOWERS

Flowers are the bloom of my heart,
Thinking of flowers reminds me of you,
As I'm wishing my flower
That we'll never be apart,
Is not so, doth I know
And then my tears fall upon you,
So beautiful but starts to wither away day after day.

Kamilah Abdelrahim (8)
Islamia Primary School

THE CRAZIEST FOOTBALL MATCH OF THE SEASON

When the match began
There was a substitution.
A free kick was given for no reason,
So they called this match the craziest match of the season.

Goalkeepers answered their mobile phones
Referees healed injured players' bones.
Players drank water when they could have scored.
So they called this match the craziest match of the season.

Injured players were forced to play,
Strikers were defending their managers
The fans had fun all day.
So they called this match the craziest match of the season.

Midfielders served the fans' meals.
Defenders were celebrating the fans.
Players then came riding horses
So they can clean the fields.
So they called this match the craziest match of the season.

Arqam Umar Ahmad (10)
Islamia Primary School

HAPPINESS

Happiness is light yellow,
It smells like sweet red roses,
Happiness tastes like fresh bread,
It sounds like someone playing trumpets,
It feels like flowers booming out,
Happiness lives at the bottom of your heart.

Yasmen Mir (9)
Islamia Primary School

WHEN I GROW OLDER, I WILL LIVE . . .

I told them:
When I grow older
I will live in the blue skies
Where I can see the stars, moon and sun

They said:
Oh, you just can't live there!

I told them:
When I grow older
I will live in the sea
Where I can swim with the dolphins and sharks
I won't live in a mansion, palace, or house

They said:
Oh, you just can't live there!

I told them:
When I grow older
I will live in the trees
Where I can fly with the owls and birds

They said:
Oh you just can't live there!

I replied to them:
Just who do you think I am?
Just a measly child, they said . . . and children like you
Should listen to their parents.

My parents don't want to understand, or listen to me.
I'll bring a Mustang into their wardrobe:

Or even better . . .
Run away to Taipei . . .
If they don't listen to me!

Mehreen Hanslot (9)
Islamia Primary School

THE WORLD

This is the world for us to live in,
We must not do bad things because it is a sin.
We must try to keep the world very clean,
And the sun is beautiful and it gleams.
The beautiful flowers that some people keep in their houses,
There are some animals that go in people's houses
And they are called mice
And when the mice are in the people's houses,
Their house gets very dirty and smelly.
So remember to keep your house and the world clean!

Zahida Ashraf (8)
Islamia Primary School

PEACE

Peace is a blessing, which God gave
Something we must treasure and save
Don't let darkness come in its way
Or there will be prices for people to pay
Let it remain in our hearts
Forever and ever
And hope that peace will bring it together.
Peace is a blessing which God gave,
So please don't let it fade away.

Asmaa Shah (9)
Islamia Primary School

WHAT I WISH FOR IN THE WORLD

I wish for the world to have no war
I wish for the world to find more methods to explore
Other than anger, violence and hatred
Let there be peace instead

If there were no war
The world could live happily ever more
I wish for peace
And all the tension to cease.

Hala Bashir (8)
Islamia Primary School

THE LIGHT OF LIFE

The stars are so bright and the sky is full of light.
The moon is shining high.
When it is sunny I am so happy.
When it is rainy I am so lazy and bored.
I like the day when it is full of light.
The sun is ever so bright.
I like the sun when it shines.
When it is snowy I always slip
But thank God for my light of life
I get up and start again.

F Nabilah El-Harraj (9)
Islamia Primary School

THE SUN

The sun is in the sky all day,
But doesn't it get time to play?
The sun shines brightly down on all the land,
Not missing out one bit of sand.
It shines down it's hot sunray,
To make the children go out and play.
It brightens our life with its beautiful light
After a cold, dark sleepy night.

Mustafa Hamid (10)
Islamia Primary School

I'D LIKE TO BE...

When I grow up,
I'd like to be...
A master of disguise,
To fight enemy spies.

When I grow up
I'd like to be...
A famous singer
Who sings,
All sorts of things.

When I grow up
I'd like to be...
A fashion designer
All dressed up
As a hard-working coal miner!

When I grow up
I'd like to be...
A person who is good
But most important
I am happy
To be me.

When I grow up
I'd like to be
Just anything
Helping others...
Some day I'll think.

Zahrah Khan (10)
Islamia Primary School

THE CAT

A cat went to town,
To buy a crown,
He wanted to sing,
To be the king,
He put the crown
That he bought from town,
On his head
And went to bed.

Miriam Ahmed (8)
Islamia Primary School

LOVE

Love is rose red,
It tastes like a fairy cake,
Love smells like freshly baked jam tarts,
Love sounds like romantic music.
It feels soft and squidgy.
Love lives in the centre of my heart.

Amir Aouf (10)
Islamia Primary School

AFTER DARK

After dark wind blows,
After dark water rumbles,
After dark ghosts creep,
After dark I hear birds singing,
After dark dogs bark,
After dark my fright runs away.

Zain Raja (9)
Islamia Primary School

FOOTBALL HERO

Just because I'm not very fast,
I get picked on the team last.
Okay, I can't dribble too well,
But I'm not completely bad like hell.
I know that football isn't my best point,
But then of course, I've got a stiff joint.
I can do a bit of goalkeeping,
Well okay, I admit a bit of weeping.
Being defender, that's totally not me,
Mustafa can do it though, maybe.
Red card, I get that a lot,
The colour of it just makes me sweat and get hot,
Abdulla, he sees the ball,
He catches it, thoughts of dumpling and all.
Everyone is jeering me by my name,
'Yusuf! Yusuf! He's so lame!'
Arqam scores, he's so proud,
Everyone is applauding really loud.
And then it is quite plain,
That our best tackler is Zain.
Midfielder has got to be Amir,
Even though he is as rough as a bear.
Suddenly, a deafening roar is heard,
'Come on Yusuf!' Hey! Have I really scored?
They used to say at football, I'm a total zero,
Now at last, I'm their football hero!

Yusuf Sherwani (9)
Islamia Primary School

FRIENDS

Friends are people you trust and like,
They are all different and don't look alike.
It's rare not to find friends not copying each other,
Or to find them giving up and saying why bother.

Friends are people you should visit on a regular basis,
Although you may get used to their same old faces.

You can play, shout and laugh a lot with them,
Go and visit places like Tower Bridge and Big Ben.
Sadly sometimes you may fight and quarrel,
But at the end of the day there's always a moral.

To be nice to your friends and get along together,
Keep in touch and always be friends forever.

Salima Boukhemia (11)
Islamia Primary School

BABIES

Babes are sweet, cuddly and pure;
But just when you're thinking they're angelic
You realise they're also smelly and gooey!
And when you have to change their nappies
You think it will be clean with nothing inside
But you are wrong, there is disgusting muck everywhere
And when they give you a kiss,
You think 'Ahhh! How clever my baby is,'
But after the kiss you find slime all over your cheek
But sometimes you are right they are sweet.

Aneesa Habaik (8)
Islamia Primary School

BEES

Bees fly in the sky
They go buzz, buzz, buzz
Bees are very active
They fly for a noble,
Bees make us honey
That is healthy for our body
And is good for money
It also tastes yummy.

Maryam Halaoui (7)
Islamia Primary School

FLOWERS

Flowers are red,
Flowers are pink,
Flowers can be any colours you think.
Flowers are green,
Flowers are blue,
Flowers can be many colours too.

Taahira Faruque (7)
Islamia Primary School

PEACE

I like to live a peaceful life
Without any war
I don't want terrorism to the poor
I don't like hijacking neither kidnapping
I want to smell fresh air
And I don't want polluted air.

Husam Hamid (9)
Islamia Primary School

11+

Eleven plus
A big fuss
It's work, work, work every day
There's no time to go out or play
Choices made
Prospectuses out laid
On the desks, on the chairs
On the beds, on the stairs
Maths, English
(Jolly selfish)
Reasoning, Deen
(They're really mean)
Twenty-four hours round the clock
If you're tired, well that's bad luck
Exam day arrives
My brain totally revives
I fly through my papers
Words pour out of my pen like vapours
'Pens down on your sheet
Exam's now complete.'

Marium Sherwani (11)
Islamia Primary School

THE FLYING BIRD

Why do birds fly high?
How do birds fly in the sky?
I wish, I wish, I wonder why!
How do birds fly so high?
Do you wonder and ponder as to why birds
Fly so high in the sky?

Amirah Anwara Abdu'Allah (8)
Islamia Primary School

SPRING

Spring's here at last,
Wonderful hot days come fast,
Roses bloom looking merry and bright,
Bathing in the golden sunlight,
The breeze rustles the bird's wing,
As the nightingales happily sing,
No longer do we see the winter and groan,
Nor hear the wind's terrible moan,
The sky is a lovely blue shade,
White clouds glide in the sky and fade,
When the sun sets all the world turns orangey red,
And children are all laid in bed,
Their eyes close while they lie,
Dreaming of buckwheat cake and pie.
Oh if only one would wake and see,
How at night stars twinkle over the sea,
Milk white moon glistening in the night,
At a great distance, a great height,
This is spring's prodigy,
This is God's blessing.

Noor Al Houda Elterk (11)
Islamia Primary School

TRUTH!

Tell the truth and make it pure,
Tell the truth and make it sure,
Tell the truth and make it your style,
Tell the truth not for a little while,

Tell the truth and make it clear,
Tell the truth and have no fear,
Tell the truth at all cost,
Tell the truth and don't be lost,

Tell the truth and let it stay,
Tell the truth every day,
Tell the truth and let it be heard,
Tell the truth whenever it occurred.

Karima Segayer (11)
Islamia Primary School

THE BOY AND THE SEA

In front of a heaving sea a boy stood
A confusing question suddenly passed his mind
He believed answering it was surely good
A sea he can see but no explanation to it he could find

The hearts and thoughts wonder about this endless blue
Who could have possibly made you?
With such a greatness which looks so true!
Magnificence and beauty which made the confusion grew

Finally the sea smiled and broke its silence
The fish living inside me are to be asked
Also the waves which are my guidance
That my heart with the love of Allah beats fast

Allah who is your God and mine
The one who protects you fine
He created you and me
No one else could it ever be

The boy waved at the sea with proudness
And with full content walked away
He expressed his happiness in loudness
Raising his hands high as he ran at the bay.

Imad el-deen Halaoui (8)
Islamia Primary School

THE WORLD TODAY

The Earth at this age is harsh and hard,
Unfortunately for Mr Bard,
He works for us to be great,
And he can't even afford a dinner plate.

Mother Nature fades away,
As coldly polluted becomes May.
Technology takes control,
As Earth loses its role.

Only few ask for peace,
While the sea bathes in grease.
The cities are filthy,
Evil people become wealthy.

Destroy devil's desire,
And extinguish the future fire.
Tie your shoe lace,
And make Earth a better place.

A noble hope meets the king,
With an important message on his wing:
'Throw away technology,
Welcome Mother Nature to rule.'

Aadil Ahmed (11)
Islamia Primary School

SCHOOL

In school we learn a lot,
From reception for learning a full stop.
In school we have time to play,
We have it in the day.

We read many a boo,
Maybe to become a famous cook.
We grow along as the years pass by,
To join some secondary school like Kingsbury High.

Muath Tawfiq (10)
Islamia Primary School

FRIENDS

I've realised who my friends are,
I was so stupid to believe
That I actually had any
I am so naïve.

I have realised what my friends are
And what exactly is a friend?
Just someone you have to believe in
A fluctuating trend.

I've realised when my friends are,
A confusion grown so tall,
With moods which change so rapidly,
You cannot really call them friends at all.

I have realised where my friends are
They exist in my mind,
The truest type of friends are they
Better than the human kind.

I guess it's just my destiny
To be a loner extraordinaire
But I believe it makes me stronger,
So happy I do not care.

Shezaad A R Raja (11)
Islamia Primary School

HELPING HANDS

Helping is something we should all do,
Being compassionate towards others,
Trying to conquer our selfishness,
Extending a hand to the needy,
Working together to produce a better world.

Achieving the best out of this life,
Assisting others worse off than us,
Relieving others of their burden,
Bringing a smile onto sad faces,
Helping each other to produce a wonderful world.

I wish the world could be peaceful,
Countries being helpful to other countries,
No war at all, no fighting at all,
Everyone just being helpful and kind,
Aiding each other to produce a superior world.

Aisha Rashid (11)
Islamia Primary School

PEACE

Peace is pure and milky white
It tastes so delicious I would love to take a bite
If every single person in the world was at peace
What a lovely sight it would be!
Everyone enjoying their own lives
Not spreading rumours and telling lies
Helping other people and those in need
Trying to cure ourselves of greed.
If every single person in the world was at peace
What a lovely sight it would be!

Siddeeqa Rashid (9)
Islamia Primary School

NATURE POEM

A flock of merry lambs come skipping by,
Swarms of bees come fluttering in the sky.

Racing through the bushes you spy the deers,
Washing under the waterfall are the little bears.

Birds chirping from the trees,
While the rabbits are nibbling fallen leaves.

As the meadows are full of fresh and green grass,
Roses growing on bushes later picked to be put in a vase.

New-born birds chirp as they try to fly with their new wings,
Their parents see their effort, happily sing.

Remember God created these beautiful things,
So we should thank him all the time.

Gofran Sawalha (10)
Islamia Primary School

PATIENCE

Patience is a special trait
That no one could ever hate
It is a special quality
Which makes a dream into reality
If we wait patiently
The rewards are unspeakable
As only one who practices patience knows
This is the secret between wisdom and truth
Patience is the backbone, which keeps us aloof
And against all odds when others are doubting
The virtue of patience is ever flouting the impatience of man.

Mahmood Sharaf (10)
Islamia Primary School

My Baby Brother

My baby brother so soft and tiny
My baby brother so clean and shiny

My baby brother will always cry
My baby brother so soft and dry

My baby brother always wants to be fed
My baby brother gets tired and goes to bed

My baby brother is very very sweet
My baby brother is so tidy and neat

My baby brother is so cute and bubbly
My baby brother so rosy and cuddly.

Zainab Rashid (8)
Islamia Primary School

Winter

Summer's gone and passed away
And now winter is on its way

How the winter is long and weary
We wish for sunshine cheery

Oh how I wish it was spring
Merrier than the winter's wing

No longer do the flowers bloom
For snow has made it as white as a moon

Oh hail stones no longer stay
That is a sign of spring on its way!

Shaymaa Sourroukh (11)
Islamia Primary School

Joy is bright blue,
It smells like a garden full of lavender,
Joy tastes like strawberry cream milkshake,
It sounds like people cheering because they passed their exams,
It feels like a round ripe plum,
Joy lives at the top of your heart.

Sarah Rhalem (9)
Islamia Primary School

MISERY

Misery is porridge grey,
It smells like rotting cabbages,
Misery tastes like gone off bread,
It sounds like a boring funeral,
Misery feels like a not working toy,
It lives in the middle of an uninteresting book.

Sumayya Ahmad (9)
Islamia Primary School

THE DEEP BLUE SEA

In the deep blue sea
The creatures swim free
The dolphin, the squid and the shark
There are other kinds of fish
As beautiful as you could wish
Who live at the bottom, in the dark.

Zahra Mughal (9)
Islamia Primary School

THE CAT

a fur ball
a football

a swishing tail
a winding trail

a slimy nose
a lady's pose

a pricked ear
a danger near

a blinking eye
a bird's cry

a silent creep
a sudden leap

a sharp claw
a gaping jaw

a flapping wing
a feline grin.

Marwa Radwan (10)
Islamia Primary School

LOVE

Love is as red as a rose,
It smells like a buttercup flower,
Love tastes red as a tart,
It feels nice and happy,
It feels soft like a banana,
Love lives in a heart.

Yasmin Hasan (10)
Islamia Primary School

TRUTH

Truth is the key,
Can't people see?
That every time we turn a corner someone lies,
Like those politicians in their ties,
The boy who cried wolf did it too,
What a joker phew!
Are white lies accepted,
Or should they be rejected?
Suspicion remains upon this land,
And lies drop out like a grain of sand,
Truth is adored with a light heart,
Which gives a nice fresh start,
It removed the guilty feeling,
Truth gives the heart a cleaning,
What is truth?
The balm that soothes,
Thank you.

Maymuna Shaheem (10)
Islamia Primary School

SCHOOL!

School is cool.
Children rule.
We do art.
Some are smart.
In every subject
We do a project.
We have break
Some have tummy ache.
Nurses cure
Teachers roar.

Sarah Sourroukh (9)
Islamia Primary School

I Wish!

I wish the world is at ease
I wish everyone lives to please
I wish everyone does one's best
For life is just a test
I wish we don't deal in bad deeds
I wish we were more generous to those with needs
I wish everyone is friend, not foe
I wish all the enmity would go
I wish for a world full of care
I wish for toleration everywhere.

Ibah Ahmad (10)
Islamia Primary School

A Volcano

A volcano is a terrible thing.
Exploding, roaring, burning.
This happened five days ago in Goma - Africa.
The red hot magma flowed down the rocky hillside
And sucked and drank in a very wicked way.
Whatever it found on its path
Thousands of people fled for their lives,
Leaving behind their houses and loving homes.
Next day they returned to find
How it swallowed their town and left its hot
Rocky footmarks everywhere.
Today the victims are queuing for food and
Crying for help.
People right now are suffering from hunger and pain.

Can you tell me how to punish a volcano?

Daniel Attiyah (9)
Lyndhurst House School

A Christmas Memory

Bells chiming clear and loud
A snowflake rests upon my nose.
The cold winter wind embraces the cathedral.
I hold on to my granny's hand.
Wishing for the big oak doors to open.
The chill begins to bite my cheeks.
When eventually heaven's gates part,
People rush to their seats.
My family and I can hear the choir singing,
'Away in a manger', an angel's voice
The Christmas trees sparkle and glitter
Looking up to the ceiling, I'm sure the angels are dancing and cheering
As the choir sings, 'Oh come all ye faithful'.
I know Christmas is here.

Alexander Allen (11)
Lyndhurst House School

Walking By The Welsh Harp On Wednesday Afternoon, 16th May

One wet, windy Wednesday
We went walking by the Welsh Harp
The fields were like carpets
Of bluebells, buttercups and daisies.
We trod through the long bulrushes
And saw tiny tadpoles in a dirty pond.
The trees were full of multicoloured blossom
And the smell of the red campion was sweet.

Toby Gould (10)
Lyndhurst House School

HOMEWORK

Homework oh homework I mess with you all night,
I throw you away,
But you're still in my sight.
It must be a punishment to have you every night,
But I still have to do you, so you're a fright,
Homework oh homework please go away.

I know you help me,
But I've been learning all day.
So homework oh homework please go away.

Two subjects a night,
What a fright.
Isn't it time we had a night off,
Maths, English, history, three times a week,
Oh no Latin has started every night this week.
So homework oh homework just go away.

When we were young, we had all the fun,
We played and laughed every night,
But now this has gone and homework has come.
Oh homework oh homework, it really is no good,
We still are young, please can we have some fun?

William Barakat (10)
Lyndhurst House School

ALLITERATION

One whiff wet whisker won a wedlock week.
Two tarnished teddies thought of a thrilling thriller.
Three tip-top tornadoes tumbled towards a tower.
Four feisty fabulous families farmed a ferocious field.
Five foreign, foxy fingers found a fat fork.

Six silly, selfish suns shined at Saturn on a sap.
Seven sandy, saucy sandals settled in Scandinavia.
Eight eager eagles ate all the elves.
Nine naughty nuns knitted a neat night-dress.
Ten talented tomcats trundled to the tea tent.

Dominic Barnard (11)
Lyndhurst House School

TREES

When they grow in wood or field,
Branches reaching to the sky,
Then they sicken, fate is sealed,
Now the trees are doomed to die,
As sharp saw blades attack with zest,
These trees must die like all the rest.

Trucks come along to take some timber,
Groves are shrinking as forests slim.
When the leaves glide to the ground,
Round and round they swirl and fall.

In the spring the buds are growing,
In the summer their glory is green,
In the autumn their true colours showing,
In the winter the twigs are bare,
A season's actions are quite divine.

Green light grows through fingerless hands,
The trunk is one large leg,
As I stare at the wonders of nature,
I feel like I'm in a new world.

Isaac Epstein (9)
Lyndhurst House School

A CITY NIGHT

One night I awoke and could not get back to sleep.
I looked out of my bedroom window and this is what I saw.

The sun was just visible beyond the horizon
Staining the sky with pink, orange and red.
In the west the moon was like a half-eaten biscuit shining in the sky.

The house opposite ours had a small pond
The sun tinted the water with crimson and gold.
The moon's reflection was in the pond
As though you could reach in the pond and take the moon out.

I opened the window and the cold wind nibbled my cheeks.
The only sound was an empty Coke can rolling down the street
The smell of meat filled the air from yesterday's barbecue.

Oliver Gafsen (9)
Lyndhurst House School

THE LEAF TITANIC

A wind is like a big wave
A leaf is like a boat sinking in the sea
Floating in the air from left to right
Up and down then the leaf softly landed on the ground
A street lamp looks like a lighthouse
Glowing in a far distance
It shows us where to go
A dust in the wind is a man in the sea
He is trying to swim in the deep sea
The rain falls and pushes everything down into the drain
And so goes the leaf Titanic.

Naoya Shimizu (9)
Lyndhurst House School

A Sailor's Tale

I sailed across the sea like a bird in flight.
About to catch its prey, which awaits its painful death.

The fishes were so huge, and as slow as a tortoise.
But they were so strong they rocked my boat like a cradle,
From one side to another, as if I were a baby being put to sleep.

The sun glittered on water's surface,
As if it were winking off a warrior's silver-plated armour.

The waves were like footballers chasing a ball
Across the big blue football pitch, and the ball was my boat!

I heard crackles in the sky from lightning,
But it sounded like a firework getting spread into the sky!

Denis Konoplev (10)
Lyndhurst House School

The Big City

The bright, shining lights
The tall buildings covering the sky line.
People rushing to go home.
The sound of car horns
With police sirens sounding,
People walking home with heavy bags.
Thieves stealing people's mobile phones.
Cars passing red lights and speeding.
Children riding their bicycles.
Children nagging their mum to go in toy stores.
The dogs barking
The sun is shining down on the big city, my big city.

Aria Khani (10)
Lyndhurst House School

IN THE MIDNIGHT MOONLIGHT

Alone in the park
As I sit on a bench,
Underneath the moonlight,
As the cold air
Pinches my cheeks
The sky is looking down at me.
Stars are shining
Like teardrops in my eyes,
The silence falls
But I want to meet someone.
Lamplights are starting to turn on
And I start to wonder
Would anybody meet me
Under the midnight moonlight?
Leaves spiralling off trees
Onto the damp and short grass.
Soon I feel lonely
Cold and sad.
I begin to ask myself
What am I doing?
I feel like I ran away
Away from my family and friends.
The clouds and stars are watching me,
Telling me to go back,
Back to my family and friends.
I cannot stop thinking,
How my family is.
I am one of them
And I feel sad,
Under the Midnight Moonlight.

Adam D Robinow (9)
Lyndhurst House School

CRICKET FANS

The officer stands
To take the ticket
As the fans come
To watch the cricket.

As the player hits
The ball in the air
It is something that
A crowd cannot bear.

And the umpire shouts
That is not fair
The crowd then sits
Down in deep despair.

At last the player
Gets himself caught out,
And from half the crowd
Rises an unhappy shout.

Then the team is out
For a poor one hundred runs
As they go in to field
They are losing by tons.

For then it is time
For the last bowl
As the ninety-seven goes to one hundred and one
The player stands up to receive his goal.

Joel Freedman (10)
Lyndhurst House School

WINTER

The trees lose their beautiful leaves
They hover down like enchanted magic carpets
Landing on their post,
The houses putting white hats on their roofs,
The parks and people's gardens all covered in a thick blanket of snow
The cats shivering, no longer play their catch the bird chasing game.
People packed in warm clothes,
The squirrels and bears about to go to sleep through the winter months
The children building cheerful looking snowmen,
Winter has taken place.

Adam Zwierzynski (11)
Lyndhurst House School

FIVE THINGS FOR CHRISTMAS

I wish to be given beautiful things this Christmas,
beautiful but impossible:
One Christmas present would be to have a baby foal as black as ebony.
My second Christmas present is to have the talent of Eidur Gudfonsons with all his skill.
The psychic powers to feel any people's feelings and to change them.
My old dog Luca. I would love to touch his silky, golden fur.
I would like to break a football record for being the best player ever.

David Khalastchi (10)
Lyndhurst House School

THE WIND

The wind brushes against the leaves.
It makes a loud whirling noise.
It sometimes can blow down trees that are big or small.
On hot, summers days it keeps us cool.

The wind is very useful.
At night, a dark wind
Eerie, cold, crashing blindly
Crackling branches
Whistling around corners unseen.

Riccardo Lara (11)
Lyndhurst House School

CHRISTMAS MEMORY

My favourite Christmas tree is the one we have at home
With the bright, white fairy lights and the little
Tin soldiers standing very straight.
The silver balls hanging from each branch
The gold fairy queen on top of the tree
Keeping watch on my family and me.
This special Christmas tree will always be in my memory.

Sam Hardcastle (10)
Lyndhurst House School

CHRISTMAS MORNING

When I looked out, I could not believe what I saw,
A huge blanket of snow had covered the cold, slippery ground.
Snowflakes drifting like doves,
Landing soft as feathers.
When I came down, glittering lights caught my eyes.
For there was the tree, standing like a beacon.
And under its branches was the real excitement.
For inside the parcels, lay the promise of joy.

Shamil Dudhia (10)
Lyndhurst House School

Jubilee In June

I can't wait till the month of June.
It will be a month with no doom or gloom;
With the English team playing in Japan,
It will be a joyous occasion for every fan.
I'm sure we can defeat Germany and Brazil,
Italy and France will be left in a trance.
In June we are given a chance
To party countrywide, celebrate and dance.
The Queen has reigned for fifty years,
And everyone should see this in joyous tears.
What is going on? What is Blair trying to prevent?
Why are we only given two days for such a big event?
The country is witnessing a golden jubilee,
And everyone needs a chance to show glee.
I think Parliament should pass a law:
That gives us all a reason to glow.
I hope the English team will do the sensible thing
And present the World Cup to the precious Queen.

David Zargaran (10)
Lyndhurst House School

A Kiwi

The brittle brown coating
Covers the unripe centre.
A prickly almost hairy feel it has.
The inside lush, green and inviting
Its seeds produce the shape of the northern star.
I long to try it.
I long to try it.

Milton Karamani (9)
Lyndhurst House School

THE SEA

The shiny water glittering or the murky water's dullness,
The sea cools you down when you go in it,
The sea frightens you when you go too far,
The fish swimming, the sleek, smooth fish darting
off into the murkiness,
The crabs burrowing into the sand,
The turtle rushing on the sand to lay their eggs before daybreak,
In the depths of the sea,
The sea is nearly black,
The shoals of fish being hunted by the predators,
Going further into the water down into the depths
where the gravity can nearly crush a person,
The sea is now consumed.

Imran Basri (10)
Lyndhurst House School

CHOCOLATE PANCAKE

Oozing out of its fried cover
Like brown lava spouting out of a volcano,
It's a mouth-tingling sensation!
Bubbling with irresistible taste.
It is as though you are in a chocolate heaven.
It smells of a rose in a summer garden.
Once finished, you wished you had some more,
Then you wait till tomorrow
And until it comes
You hang your head in sorrow.

Kunal Choraria (10)
Lyndhurst House School

DEEP BLUE SEA

The silent world not so silent
Fish zoom in and out of the algae
The parrotfish imitate everyone
The dolphins chirp and click affectionately
The tuna school swims lazily around
The eels lie in secret waiting to pounce
The big whale yawns day and night
The stingrays lie in the sand unnoticed
The killer whale's intelligent head is hungry for food
The butterfly fish swims delicately around its home
The giant clams bite and chomp ferociously
The sardines packed together tightly
The flying fish jump in and out of the sea
The silent world not so silent.

Samuel Taylor (10)
Lyndhurst House School

A CITY NIGHT

One night when I couldn't go to bed,
I went to see what was outside.
So I crept out to the balcony to look.
Outside was silent.
I saw millions of stars and a half-eaten biscuit.
The noise I could hear was the wind hitting trees.
I felt the wind rushing to my face as if it were drunk.
The wind still smelled of pizzas from Pizza Hut.
This reminded me how hungry I was,
So I asked my mum for a night snack.

Yuki Oka (9)
Lyndhurst House School

Winter Night Is Gone

The cold winter wind of the night
Gently brushing the back of my neck,
The brightly lit blaze of the warm fireplace
My dog running, howling in the bitter night air,
But what is this to me?
A little dot revolving round and round in my head.
The blown out fire, ashes scattered
Where is the winter wind?
Whirling through the misty air.
But what is this to me?
Nothing any more.

Justen Barget (10)
Lyndhurst House School

The M-26 Falcon Aircraft

It is as fast as a Concorde,
It even sounds like eagles screeching.
It can blast a tank
With its typhoon missiles,
Firing like launched torpedoes.
It has the wings of diving falcons.
As long as a limo
And its beak is a pencil's sharpened tip.
It has beautiful, shiny armour,
But most of all,
It bears the symbol of the RAF.

Aryan Alipour (10)
Lyndhurst House School

A Centaur

A half-man, half-horse comes
Out from the forest, his powerful
Legs make the ground shake with
Fear. His long beard touches the
Ground. His hot breath makes
The air hot. He hunts the goats
Like a lioness hunts a zebra as
Quiet as a feather and as fast as
A rocket. He lives in the most
Darkened places in the forest.
His horseshoes blaze with
Fire when the sun rises over
The forest. Sometimes the Centaur
Waits for its victim and when you
Blink you see no victim and then
Suddenly you can hear a
Roaring and tearing noise
Every single animal in the
Forest fears the Centaur
Because he is the most horrible
And furious animal in the books
The young Centaurs are very beautiful
But very dangerous. The old ones look ugly
And very weak in Hercules times there
Was a legend that Hercules fought the Centaur
And after a fierce fight Hercules won, but the Centaur
Became friends with Hercules.

Ben Rabinovich (10)
Lyndhurst House School

THE WIND

The wind is a type of
Powerful force that sweeps
The leaves up and down,
As though being shot and
Then falling to their death.
The wind seeks many places
It likes going into corners
Like a vacuum cleaner
And sucks the dust or earth
Out of its hiding place.
Soon it comes and then
Beware before it blows
You away!

Chris Cronin (10)
Lyndhurst House School

FOOTBALL

A football is like The Millennium Wheel
With its black and white stripes.
It spins like a fan
The wind blowing against your face.
A football is black and white,
Like a beautiful sketch.
When you are sad
A football cheers you up.
When it strikes you
Then it is your enemy.
A football is round like an orange
A football is a flying carpet.

Mark Keisner (10)
Lyndhurst House School

BLUE

Blue is the colour of the beautiful calm sea
Blue is the colour of a wonderful clear, cloudless sky
Blue is the rain on a rainy day
Blue is how I feel when I feel down.

Blue is the first thing on my mind when sadness appears
Blue is the colour when a new day comes
Blue is the colour of my old, comfy jeans
Blue is the royal of the spectrum.

Blue is the colour of the juicy, ripe blueberries
Blue is the colour of the sweet-smelling hyacinths in bloom
Blue is the colour of my bright, inquisitive eyes
Blue is the mess of the ink splattered across the page.

Adam Barget (9)
Lyndhurst House School

LEAVES

The leaves plunging to their death
Sailing down like a plane.
Dropping on the ground,
People stepping on them
The dustman comes,
He rakes them into a pile
He piles them up,
Then drops them in the bin.

David Keisner (10)
Lyndhurst House School

SNOW

Snow is a cold layer of wool.
It comes floating to the ground,
When it falls on you, you get a shiver
Like when you are scared.

When the snow comes drifting down,
The grass is no longer green.
The thick whiteness of snow has coated
The roofs, trees and earth.
It is a very white Christmas.
The trees are naked,
For the leaves have gone and the town is very quiet.

Oliver Sharpstone (10)
Lyndhurst House School

CERBERUS

The dog of Hell is here!
Its fiery eyes and bloodthirsty mouth,
Guarding the entrance of the dead,
Making the ground rumble when it moves
The terrible howl freezing those who are near,
And biting, tearing and eating up all in view
Its claws even tearing steel,
As he slowly goes to sleep the poem has to end,
But wait! There is one more thing to know,
This dog's bite is worse than its bark!

Kevin Tan (10)
Lyndhurst House School

DINO EGG

I don't know what it is but it is in its egg
Only his legs and hands show, they are light yellow.
It is a little animal, small as a mouse
It squeaks so lightly, I can hardly hear it.
It is very cute even though I can't see its face,
I can't wait until it hatches.

Nikola Govedarica (11)
Lyndhurst House School

MY VIEW OF RED

Red is a flame burning hot
Starting to melt my shiny pot.
Red is a bull's destination
Chasing all day the bus station.
Red is the shadow standing beside me
Running all day he allows me.
Red is the girl of my dreams
Walking with me beside the streams.
Red is the colour I see
Buzzing all day like a bee.
Red is the daunting face I see
He's not so sure about you or me.
Red is the colour of my favourite team
They always win in my mysterious dreams.
Red is the feeling I get when I score
The other team wish they were on tour.
Red is the colour of my heart
Thank you for reading my part.

Bar Hariely (9)
Mathilda Marks-Kennedy School

A MIXTURE OF GOOD/BAD DAYS

I remember when I first went to the beach
The waves were roaring like tigers
Splashing so high when the sun was setting
I remember when I first went to France.
The men were singing like songbirds.
It had a fun garden that I got lost in.
Do you remember your good day?
I remember when I was running and someone tripped me up.
I went flying like a rocket taking off.
I remember when my brother took my chocolate
And he hid it in his pocket with cheeky smile on his face.
Mum found it in the washing machine.
All gooey and soft.
Mum shouted at me
'Do you remember your bad day?'

Nadav Albin (8)
Mathilda Marks-Kennedy School

THE SHADOW

The shadow is in front of the sun as it rises.
It moves slowly, softly and quietly
I can just hear the footsteps go by
It is dark and gloomy
It looks like me
But that is all I can see
When I move
It stands as still as a rock
And that is The Shadow.

Amy Boekstein (7)
Mathilda Marks-Kennedy School

THE BIG DAY

The big day had arrived.
Hallelujah! Their taxi has come,
Mr MacLiver,
He drove us to the airport.
We put our stuff in the boot
We found a lot of soot,
Mr MacLiver,
He drove us to the airport,
We got on the plane,
And started to play our game,
Mr MacLiver,
He drove us to the airport.
We started to fly,
My sister started to cry
Mr MacLiver
He drove us to the airport.
We went up very high
We hoped it would be a fun flight,
Mr MacLiver,
He drove us to the airport.
We finally got down,
And my sister fell down,
Mr MacLiver,
He drove us to the airport.

Sophie Mattes (10)
Mathilda Marks-Kennedy School

A COLD, WINTER'S DAY

Snow falling, snow falling
On a cold, winter's day.
Can you hear the snow falling
On the cold, icy ground?

Pitter-patter, pitter-patter go the soft snowflakes
Whoosh, whoosh, whoo goes the blazing, cold wind
Snow falling, snow falling
On a cold, winter's day.

Natasha Pein (8)
Mathilda Marks-Kennedy School

DOWNSTAIRS AT NIGHT

Wake up feeling hungry
Or maybe thirsty.
Slip the slippers on
Go downstairs
Creak, creak
Tell the floor to shut up.
Still hungry
Still thirsty.

Into the kitchen
Reach for a cup.
Open the wrong cupboard
Clink, clank
Shhhhhhh!

Put the pans back
Open the right cupboard
Take a cup.
Take the milkshake
Pour it in the cup, taste it . . .
Oh no . . . it's soy sauce!
Pour milkshake in
Drink . . .
Mission accomplished!

Adam Lewis (11)
Mathilda Marks-Kennedy School

RED

Red is a devil, flaming hot
Red is burning my lovely pot
Red is wine makes me drunk
The next day I see a read-headed punk.

Red is fire mixed with yellow
Then I feel all red Jell-O
Red is all around me filled with anger
It always gets louder and louder.

Red is a heart
Red is sweet
But red is Man U
My sisters want to meet.

Red is chicken pox
That is red
It's time to go to bed!
That's my red.

Jonathan Black (8)
Mathilda Marks-Kennedy School

THIS IS FOOTBALL

This is football!
The crowds' emotion goes up
The players start the match
And Beckham on the right goes for a shot
Ohhh, he missed
This is football!

Elliot Zabaroff (10)
Mathilda Marks-Kennedy School

GREEN IS

Green is grasshoppers hopping,
Green is grass waving like saying hi.

Green is trees standing upright,
Almost touching the sky.

Green is mint toothpaste to clean your teeth,
Green is a frog all slimy and warty.

Green is poison,
All scary and naughty.

Green is pineapples,
Hanging from trees.

When you fall over, green is the
Colour on your trouser knees.

Joshua Goodman (9)
Mathilda Marks-Kennedy School

IN A DARK, SPOOKY NIGHT

In a dark, spooky night
I had a very big fright!
There was a ghost in my dream.
It led me into a spooky castle!
Then into a pitch-dark room,
The light turned on.
It was a room full of ghosts!
At least there was a box
In the middle of the room
It led me out.

Nadav Ezra (7)
Mathilda Marks-Kennedy School

THE FOUR SEASONS

In winter the morning is cold and dark
It is breezy, you can hear the trees blowing.

In spring when you're inside your house
You can hear the rain pattering on the windows.

In spring when the sun is shining and you're in the garden
The sun shines on your face.

In autumn when you are walking along
You can hear the leaves rustling.
They crackle and crunch all over
When it is sunny and you are in a garden and you are having lunch
It's sometimes so sunny you go under a tree.

It's summer
The sun is shining
You have a cold drink to cool you down
You are not so hot and bothered now.

Elana Freeman (7)
Mathilda Marks-Kennedy School

WHAT IS GREEN?

Green is a frog, while it jumps in the air.
Green leaves, falling out the trees.
Green is a crocodile, biting your leg off.
Trees, tall green trees taller than you.
Toothpaste, small, soggy toothpaste, nice and thin.
Grass, long and bendy, bright green like a pen.
A grasshopper, changing colours like you've never seen before.
Green.

Claudia Stone (9)
Mathilda Marks-Kennedy School

THE PUPPY IS ALONE

There was a little Dalmatian,
Waiting for his best friend called Mark
The Dalmatian had bright, sparkly eye-catching black spots.

He was crying and his eye drops,
Are making puddles on the hard, brown, bright floors,
His water puddles were going on another floor and another floor
The postman came and put some letters in
And the dog was so happy
But it wasn't his best friend
He was so cross that he fell back.

The Dalmatian was waiting for one hour and a half
He was going to sleep then he was fast asleep
His best friend came home from school
The puppy was so happy that he wagged his tail
And they played together.

Liron Mannie (7)
Mathilda Marks-Kennedy School

MEMORIES

I remember when I played the guitar sounds out of the window
My family singing with me, I felt warm.

I remember me playing with my friends, having a beautiful time.
Running in the playground, I felt happy.

I remember when I was in nursery, having fun with my friends.
I felt shy of the teacher.

I remember my last day or nursery, I felt very sad.
What do you remember?

Daniel Brovman (7)
Mathilda Marks-Kennedy School

Yellow Is...

Yellow is like a big yellow and orange sun
Leaping over the blue and yellow and big shady, green sea.
A big sunflower as tall as me with soft petals that's like silk.
A small, little chick that's just been born
Sucking from its mum, crying that it's unsure.
A fat pineapple that's got spikes.
You prick yourself.
Big, juicy banana that I like to suck
Yum, yum, pull the skin off, use my nail duck.

Gabriella Mannie (9)
Mathilda Marks-Kennedy School

What Can't You Hear?

Can you hear the sun going up?
Can you hear the owl flying in the night?
Can you hear the ghost going through the wall?
Can you hear them?
Be quiet and you might.

Jordan Ezekiel (8)
Mathilda Marks-Kennedy School

My Little Sister

I can hear my sister
Laughing, giggling, running in the house.
I throw a ball
She rolls it back
I get a teddy
She hugs it so tight.

Aden Amsellem (8)
Mathilda Marks-Kennedy School

WHAT IS WHITE?

White is the snow falling down in the winter,
White is the colour of the stars out at midnight,
Don't forget the moon as a cookie high up in the sky!
White is some ice in a drink of Coke,
White is a glass of milk full of calcium,
White is a cloud high up in the sky during the winter,
White is the colour of your face when you're about to faint,
White could always be some silky, white paint!
White could also be a cover for a book!

Ruby Moss (8)
Mathilda Marks-Kennedy School

WHITE

White is the colour of snow in winter,
White is the colour of ice, it's a dazzling colour
That shines with the sun beating down on top of it.
White is the colour of a ghost shrieking and hovering over you.
White is the colour of a child's pale face.
White is the colour of paper and the clouds.
White is a beautiful colour!

Rachel Barnberg (8)
Mathilda Marks-Kennedy School

THE OPPOSITES

An opposite is like up and down.
There are different opposites.
There is stand and sit,
Grow and shrink.
These are opposites.

Yoav Greenberg (7)
Mathilda Marks-Kennedy School

THE TRAMP!

Don't go near that mean old man,
You should never ever be his fan.
Do you know who I'm talking about?
It's old Jack Rugs!

Do you think he's nice or mean?
He's the ugliest tramp you've ever seen!
Do you know who I'm talking about?
Oh, old Jack Rugs!

Don't look at him, he's so mean,
And was never in his life 'clean'!
Do you know who I'm talking about?
He's old Jack Rugs!

But how do you think he should feel?
He's being killed and eaten like a meal.
Do you know who I'm talking about?
Poor old Jack Rugs!

Danielle Michelson (10)
Mathilda Marks Kennedy School

MY DOG IN THE PARK

My dog has lots of friends.
She plays and fights playfully
She comes and plays with me.
I play with her on the grass,
She follows me around
She goes home with me
She goes to sleep on my bed
Goodnight Phoebe.

Maya Solnitzky (8)
Mathilda Marks-Kennedy School

THE SINGLE TREE

One tree stands all alone,
It grows so silently,
No one cars for it, yet it lives,
In spring it grows new buds
And becomes bright and beautiful.

One tree stands all alone,
It grows so silently.
In summer its buds turn to blossom,
Its leaves rustle in the breeze
Enjoying the warmth of the sun.

One tree stands all alone,
It grows so silently.
In autumn its beauty dies,
Green becomes brown
And falls to the ground.

One tree stands all alone,
It grows so silently
In winter the branches are bare,
Fighting through the snow
To reach another spring.

Lauren Lightstone (10)
Mathilda Marks Kennedy School

BLACK

Black is a colour of a daunting beetle.
Black is a zoom through the sky.
Black is a colour of an ant in danger.
Black is a dark room where someone is asleep.
Black is a colour of someone's hair.

Ben Goldberg (9)
Mathilda Marks-Kennedy School

YELLOW

Yellow
Yellow is so shiny and hot,
Like a little baby warm in its cot.
It's yellow like a sunflower,
As tall as the Eiffel Tower.
Yellow is when the sun goes up,
It's like lemonade you pour in a cup.
Sand is yellow too,
In the beach around you.
Yellow in traffic lights,
Yellow is bright and new,
Look around and see maybe it's
Behind you!

Zoe Ilivitzky (9)
Mathilda Marks-Kennedy School

MY SISTER

My sister is crying
Can you hear her?
My sister is running
Can you hear her?
My sister is colouring
Can you hear her?
My sister is eating
Can you hear her?
My sister is talking
Can you hear her?
I love listening to her
I love watching her.

Tomm Shkoury (8)
Mathilda Marks-Kennedy School

BLOODY DECISION!

He freezes still
The decision awaits him,
Should he give up this idea of
Declaring and winning war?
We'd never know -
Only the teacup in which he made
His decision filled up to the brim
For some it is too late to part
In the election it's his own fault.
The blood of his people rolls down his cheeks.
The election that holds his future
People with a mutter -
His own idea will not matter!

Talya Robinson (10)
Mathilda Marks-Kennedy School

WHAT IS YELLOW?

Yellow is the sun rising in the colourful world.
Yellow is the exciting Simpson's skin,
Even the Asian people's skin is yellow,
Yellow is a sunflower growing in my garden,
Ouch I slipped on a yellow banana skin,
Ah isn't it great that we're in the yellow, deep sand,
Um that yellow cheesecake with:
Yellow mustard
Yellow banana
Yellow lemon
Yellow is the colour of happiness.

Noga Livne (8)
Mathilda Marks-Kennedy School

The Storm

Normal day at school
Trying not to act the fool
Looking out the window to see
Is there inspiration for me?

Following the trail to the mystery storm
Hoping it will hit the school lawn
Thinking of the devastation it will cause
Looking at the rain as it pours

Maybe it will soak the headmistress
Maybe it will cause complete distress
For the children who have come to play
This is never going to be a normal day

The teacher comes in and starts to shout
Is it time to leave, should we all get out?
The announcement is given we all have to leave
The storm is on its way and begins to weave.

Michael Obadia (10)
Mathilda Marks Kennedy School

I Feel Everything

I feel the wind blowing around me
I feel the rain washing my face
I feel the leaves falling on the ground
I feel the lightning striking me
I feel the storms coming into my ears
I feel alive.

Harriet Strauss (7)
Mathilda Marks-Kennedy School

THE DISMAL DAY

The dismal day was so ferocious,
And the weather was quite atrocious.
Although the sun was shining,
The rain was really really fighting.
Oh, the dismal day.

We hated the falling snow,
No one even gave it a blow.
The hailstones were clattering
With some noise and with some might.
Oh, the dismal day.

The thunder was shocking,
The lightning was mocking.
It was finally the end
Of the dismal day,
Oh do not ever fight again.

Jonathan Artman (10)
Mathilda Marks Kennedy School

BLACK

Black is a beetle running across the bath.
Black is a dark, scary night.
Black is a horrible, smelly sewer.
Black is the sticky dirt on the ground.
Black is the colour of silky, black hair.
Black is the dark floorboards creaking.
Black is colour when you close your eyes.
Black is the colour of scary bats.
Black is the colour of a lead in a pencil.

Gaby Levey (8)
Mathilda Marks-Kennedy School

GREEN

Green is the colour of trees,
It's not too harsh like a bee
The leaves sway and fall,
Like a big, bouncy ball.
Grass is tall and long,
It's a tune for a song
A frog jumps up and down,
Like a silly clown.
A crocodile starts to bite and snap,
While a butterfly starts to flap.
A grasshopper wiggles about
And you look over and see a pig's snout.
You have mint toothpaste,
It's so hot for you so you start to get chased
Apple is a fruit
It's smaller than a man's suit.

Rishana Hikmet (9)
Mathilda Marks-Kennedy School

MY BIG BROTHER

I hear pencils writing next door
Coming back from exams
Studying
Maybe I will do the same
One day
But I don't really know.
My big brother is having lots of exams
I hardly get to see him.

Louis Grant (8)
Mathilda Marks-Kennedy School

A SPOOKY, SCARY NIGHT

A spooky, scary night
When all the lights are out
The neighbours are all sleeping and no one is about.
The moon is up
And the sun is down
You're locked in a haunted house
It is pitch-dark inside.
There's a frightening ghost around
The owls' eyes are shining
And you can hear them hooting
There are very loud noises
The wind is blowing
The windows are shaking
And you're lying on your bed quaking.

Gavin Fox (8)
Mathilda Marks-Kennedy School

WHITE

White is the colour of winter, cold
It makes you shiver,
White is a snow fight,
You stop like a block of ice in wintertime.
White is a cloud up high in the sky,
And in the distance are mountains covered in snow
Above is Santa Claus saying, 'Ho, ho, ho!'
White is paper that I write on at dawn.
White is the colour of fainting,
Your face as pale as a white whale.

Libby Morris (8)
Mathilda Marks-Kennedy School

I WISH I . . .

I wish I got hard work
And didn't have a skirt
And didn't have a skirt.

I wish I was a doctor
Or a helicopter
Or a helicopter.

I wish I read all day
And went to school on Monday
And went to school on Monday.

I wish I was a volcanologist
And had a big list
And had a big list.

I wish I didn't have annoying brothers
Who shouted at their mothers
Who shouted at their mothers.

I wish I was a lot of things
And could tie all my problems up with strings
And could tie all my problems up with strings.

Shir Shafran (10)
Mathilda Marks Kennedy School

BLUE

B lue is my favourite colour,
L ight, dark, royal or electric blue.
U nder water, you can see so much blue it goes on and on,
E ven if you look up there is blue because of the sky!

So blue is used all the time, it is a great colour and the best!

Daniel Lester (8)
Mathilda Marks-Kennedy School

THE TREE

The old scrubby branches fold gently
Over the mysterious tree
And all you can see all the creatures
From branch to branch flee
The fragile leaves as light as feathers
Flow like shallow streams
They shoot like green coloured laser beams.

The roots spring through the earth
Like witty curled spines
They look as if they're humans
Without any eyes
Colourful blossoms spring up in this
Special piece of land
They're almost like a bunch of old
Tangled up elastic bands.

They move everywhere as if they're free
In my mind that's what I imagine and I can see.
Trees are a circle of our chances to survive.
Without any trees we wouldn't have a life.

Gil Albin (11)
Mathilda Marks Kennedy School

THE SEA

Do you hear the song of the sea?
It sounds so sweet.
Do you see the fish in colours blue and pink?
Don't you think the sea is beautiful, more than the sky?
Do you think the sea is blue, when the waves jump high?
I love the sea so much, don't you?

Laura Nouriel (7)
Mathilda Marks-Kennedy School

MEMORIES

I remember my first day of nursery
I felt shy and lonely but when the children saw me
They made me feel like home.

I remember my birthday, the teachers played a funny song
But the best thing was we had chocolate stars.

I remember making a pasta necklace and painting a fluffy cloud
Colouring an elegant snail and caring for my friends.

The last thing I remember is my last day of nursery
I didn't want to go home but now I've waited seven years
But I'm feeling happy cos now I'm with my friends
But they are a bit older.

Natasha Berg (7)
Mathilda Marks-Kennedy School

WHAT IS GREEN?

Green is the hill high and steep.
Sometimes your face turns *green* when you have a stomach ache.
Green is the grass, lush and long.
A stalk holding a flower is *green*.
A chameleon on grass is *green* too.
A wheelbarrow is *green* what is inside it bricks and stones.
Green is also slime in a bin. Lizard, snake, caterpillar *green*
Bounce goes a *green* frog croaking in a lake.
A jewel and a cucumber are *green*.
Green is curtain, green is a mat
Green is a balloon round and fat.
Green is the best colour of all, but
Imagine if we had no *green* in this world at all.

Tamir Chitiyat (8)
Mathilda Marks-Kennedy School

I Wish!

I wish I could have a mountain bike,
I wish I could have a pool,
I wish I could have a bowling strike,
I wish I wasn't at school.

I wish I could go to New York City,
But my parents won't let me so what a pity.
I wish I could go to Hollywood,
And eat all the tasty food.

All of those things I said are true,
So please God make all my dreams come true.

Moty Shemtov (10)
Mathilda Marks Kennedy School

The Zoo

Full of animals
Of all different types
Scary ones,
Striped ones,
Spotted ones, rare ones,
However, it could be a torturous place,
A place where you're put in a cage and
Get pointed at and laughed at,
A place where you're put on display,
A place where you're not free,
A place where you long for the day
Of your liberation of this torturous life
But it never comes.

Michael Kosky (10)
Mathilda Marks-Kennedy School

THAT'S MR WOBBLE

Mr Wobble was no bigger than a fig
He wore a mushed peas coloured wig.
    That's Mr Wobble

He wears his sharp black suit
When he picks it up from the dry cleaners
He folds it neatly in his boot
The suit is always too big,
For Mr Wobble is no bigger than a fig
    That's Mr Wobble

His toothbrush moustache that tickles his wife's face
Whilst she wears her apron made of lace
He reaches up to her knee
Because Mr Wobble is no bigger than a fig
And wears his mushed peas coloured wig
    That's Mr Wobble

He lies down on the sofa
In his sharp black suit
Which he just took from his boot
His wife sitting next to him
Laughing because his moustache tickles her face
As she takes off her apron made of lace
    That's Mr Wobble

The music blaring from his room
The swooshing from the broom
Whilst he lies down on the sofa
Stiff in his sharp black suit
Which he had in his boot
His wife downstairs so the moustache can't tickle her face
Not wearing her apron made from lace
Still Mr Wobble is no bigger than a fig
Wearing his mushed peas coloured wig
    That's Mr Wobble.

Nicola Boekstein (10)
Mathilda Marks Kennedy School

A SPOOKY, DARK HOUSE

When the sun has gone down
And the moon has gone up
A house, a spooky house
With a spooky house there's lots and lots of ghosts
And lots and lots of spiders
And no one lives there
I feel the lightning striking down
When people go in
The spiders jump
And the ghosts scare the people
Boo! I run.

Jake Mimoni (8)
Mathilda Marks-Kennedy School

TEA WITH THE QUEEN

I wore my pretty pink frock,
With a lovely big rock,
Tea with the Queen.

I put on my big blue hat,
As my cat jumped off my lap,
Tea with the Queen.

I got into the car,
It was very far,
Tea with the Queen.

I got out,
Mum gave me a shout,
Tea with the Queen.

I ate lots of cake,
It was very late,
Tea with the Queen.

When I went home, I went to bed,
And then I said goodnight to Ted,
Tea with the Queen.

Alisa Sacofsky (10)
Mathilda Marks Kennedy School

FISH IN THE SEA

If you dive straight down under the water,
You'll find fish of every kind.
Sharks, dolphins, whales,
And all kinds of other fish.

When you go further down,
You see fish that you can eat.
Like salmon, cod, haddock,
And huge shoals of tuna.

Fish do a lot to humans
And to the Earth.
Fish also get eaten by
Bigger fish.

Robert Lewis (7)
Mathilda Marks-Kennedy School

THE SEA

The crash of the waves against the cliff wall,
The noisy sky with the seagulls' call,
The pitter-patter as the rain starts to fall,
These are sounds from a wet, wet seashore.

A clap of thunder with the lightning too,
Play on the beach? That's what you can't do.
Everyone had hoped for a sunny day,
But it's a stormy day in the month of May.

Unfortunately, it's a windy day too,
But wait - have I spoken too soon?
The wind is blowing the clouds away,
And the sun's coming out to brighten the day.

The weather is good like it should be in May.
As all the children come out to play,
The one mood around is joy,
It's coming from every girl and boy.

The sounds of the moving toys,
The shouts and screams from girls and boys,
The moving and gentle sounding tide,
These are the sounds echoing far and wide.

Jacob Hilton (11)
Mathilda Marks-Kennedy School

THE WORLD IS WHITE

White is the colour when you are about to faint,
White is the colour of a pot of white paint.
Look into the sky you might see a white cloud,
Step outside there might be snow on the ground.
Water in coldness will turn into ice,
You can write on paper, that's something white.
In the middle of the water there's a gang of white swans,
There are the cheerleaders holding white pom-poms.
If you brush your teeth they'll stay bright white,
If you see a ghost he'll give you a fright.
The moon is white and shines at night,
If you see a bride she'll be dressed in white.
Look at the milk in the see-through glass,
A poem about white, to do in class.

Deborah Elf (8)
Mathilda Marks-Kennedy School

BABY'S FIRST WORD

Moo
Oh you are trying to be a cow?
Ma-Ma
Well done, I always knew I would be your first word.
Mo
Sorry what did you say?
Me
Yes, you, of course it's you!
Mmmmore
Here you go.

Adam Mimoni (10)
Mathilda Marks-Kennedy School

BLACK

Black is a colour shading dark.
Black is the colour of the sky.
I don't know why!

Black is the cat sitting on the wall
Like I sit playing chess in the hall.
Black is my queen, I make a move,
I hope I don't lose.
Black is my mood when I lose, I stamp my shoes.

Black glows at night the time for no light
I shut my eyes.
Black is the darkest of them all
It's so cool.

Joshua Jacobs (8)
Mathilda Marks-Kennedy School

TREES

Leaves are red even
Sometimes brown or green.
The trunk is long and curved
And brown.
The branches are wavy,
Like a snake when it
Moves around, around.
You can plant a seed
And it grows into a tree.

The roots are wavy,
Like a girl when
She moves her arm.
Around, around.

Gemma Ashken (10)
Mathilda Marks Kennedy School

SOME THINGS THAT ARE RED

Red are roses that make up posies,
Some cherries are *red*, that's what I said
What is better to post my letter,
Than a box that is *red*
Like the cap on my head?

Strawberries, plums and grapes,
Are *red* fruits that come in different shapes,
In fact, some grapes are so fine
They are made into *red* wine.

When it's cold outside
And full of snow,
Red cheeks give a rosy glow.
Red is blood that can run like a flood,
When I stand on my head
It makes my face *red*.

At the end of the day
When the sun is no longer high,
There is a lovely *red* tinge in the evening sky.

Nathan Pomerance (8)
Mathilda Marks-Kennedy School

WHAT IS RED?

Red is many different things,
And has meanings too.
It stands for danger and for rage
And it doesn't look like blue.

It's a primary colour,
And can be mixed with yellow and blue.
Red is the colour of blood
And it's also a sunset for you.

Red is the colour for Christmas,
And also of beautiful berries,
It's always a fun time for kids,
With all those yummy cherries.

Red is not my favourite colour,
But it is very important,
And so I do wonder,
Why it is so silent?

Gideon Caplin (9)
Mathilda Marks-Kennedy School

SPIDER!

She rests her cheek on
The cool, clear glass, the harsh frame.
A... 'something' creeps near.

A small, round, black... thing.
Eight legs, loping crawl,
It inches closer.

It came from the frame,
It had been there by her all along,
As she leant.

It did not harm her,
When of it she was unconscious,
When she sees it, she fears.

It did not harm her when,
Of the spider she was unaware,
How can it bite when she knows it is there?

Rachel Schraer (10)
Mathilda Marks-Kennedy School

SAVE THE ANIMALS

Stealthily he creeps towards the lion.
Slowly he reaches out with his gun.
Suddenly bang!

Then all goes quiet, but no.
Footsteps, a trail of blood
And a lion skin
Slung over the back
Of a tall thin man.

This man is cold.
His coat will be
Warm with the
Skin of the lion.

To kill the animals is
Insane. Please let it
Never happen again. So
Just save the animals!

Yael Shafritz (10)
Mathilda Marks Kennedy School

WHAT IS YELLOW?

Yellow is the colour of the sunset coming down
It's so beautiful
I don't think you will ever frown
Yellow is the colour of a sweet baby chick
Yellow is the colour of the Simpsons having a dip.
In the water lies a quarter of yellow fish
And yellow snakes saying hiss!

Shira Mass (8)
Mathilda Marks-Kennedy School

THE TYRE

There was a tyre
In a dump it humped and bumped.
Kids took it to play.
The tyre.

It was a dirty tyre
A muddy one too,
It rolled out of the dump
Like a football too.
The tyre.

One kid took it to play
He used it every day
It bounced and played.
The tyre.

The last day he played
With his tyre he was sad
Because of the wire
Which burst his tyre.
The tyre.

He put it back in the dump
That was the last day
He saw his black lump
Of rubber.
The tyre.

Marcus Freeman (10)
Mathilda Marks Kennedy School

WHEN I WAS BORN

Mum and Dad
Were very glad
That I was born.

They gave me a name,
Which was terribly insane,
When I was born.

My grandma thought that I was a boy,
But the rest gave me a toy,
When I was born.

After a few weeks, I took my first step,
And moved into a house that was for let,
After I was born.

I started crying,
My parents kept trying,
When I was born.

I said my first word,
And everyone heard,
After I was born.

Then my mummy,
Had a big tummy
After I was born.

I saw my new baby,
So I went crazy,
When she was born.

And now I'm big
And a very clever kid,
After I was born.

Ronelle Lang (10)
Mathilda Marks Kennedy School

WHAT IS GREEN?

As green as a scaly crocodile or a newborn duckling.
As green as swirling green leaves in autumn
Or mint toothpaste swishing around in your mouth.
As green as camouflaged tanks shooting rapidly into the enemy
As green as an extinct, ferocious dinosaur
Or grass swaying peacefully in a meadow.
As green as a cool cucumber
Or strange as broccoli or as stringy as celery
Green, this is what green is . . .

Daniel Cohen (9)
Mathilda Marks-Kennedy School

MEMORIES

I remember, I remember
When I used to write songs
And sing them. Will I be a singer one day?

I remember, I remember
My first word as a baby
It wasn't mummy or daddy
It was camera!

I remember, I remember
When I lived in Manchester
I was caught on my own shopping for sweets

I remember, I remember
When I came to London
I was sick
My dad made a bed in the car.

Pooja Varsani (9)
Roe Green Junior School

RAINBOW COLOURS

I sleep in my bed
The colour is red

I stay with a fellow
And he is yellow

I have a stink
And he is pink

I've seen a bean
That is green

I've seen a circle
And it is purple

I've got an orange
That is orange

I've got a clue
It is blue.

Sarah Pirbhai (8)
Roe Green Junior School

COMING ALIVE

Lazy red buses sleeping,
A silver water fountain whispering,
A metal gate creaking open,
A spooky camera spying,
A creepy bench wobbling,
A massive tree whispering in the wind,
A long lamp post shining brightly,
A thorny bush stinging everyone who came by.

Aroshana Haththotuwa (10)
Roe Green Junior School

HIDDEN TREASURE

When I was a little girl
All I could say was
Mamma and dada
Then I grew older

I could say
Longer words
I could understand them

I could use them in a better way
Making longer sentences
And hold my own
This at times got me in trouble
By being naughty to people.

Charlote Aguallo (10)
Roe Green Junior School

BRING THINGS ALIVE

Green gardens fast asleep,
White cameras spying on me,
The silver water fountain whispering,
Square glass windows smirking,
Green doors opening and closing,
Bare tree branches dancing,
The entrance doors swinging,
The full shelter with a stomach ache,
Round steps walking with care,
Brick chimney smoking.

Jaina Patel (10)
Roe Green Junior School

HIDDEN TREASURE

Hidden it is, but easy to find
Deep inside a human mind
For there is one boy
Who is not so kind
And always in a horrid wind

One fine day
On a Saturday
The boy went out to play

Then out came his mum
And gently rubbed his tum
And said 'Are you hungry today?'

'No' he said
And hit her head
'What a horrible mum you are
You are much worse than a star'

She wept in tears
But let out her fears
'What an unthoughtful boy you are
Your goodness is so hard to find
Sometimes you can be so kind'
Listening to Mum made him feel so bad
And decided to make it up to her
'I promise on the world of my dad
From now I'll be a good lad'
So from that day on he was so kind.

Sinthuja Subashkaran (9)
Roe Green Junior School

I Remember, I Remember

I remember, I remember . . .
a red and white tricycle fast and shiny.

I remember, I remember . . .
learning to walk back and forth all the time.

I remember, I remember . . .
my blue, fluffy teddy ripped by my brother.

I remember, I remember . . .
saying my first word when I was two.

I remember, I remember . . .
my first sip of Sprite and my first lick of ice cream.

Nikhil Savani (9)
Roe Green Junior School

Coming Alive

Sprinkling fountains whispering quietly.
Tall red buses roaring down the street.
Thundering lightning soaring through the sky.
Rustling green grass swishing violently.
Big black ravens circling the sky.
Two big basketball nets boringly standing there.
Spooky cameras spying upon playing children.
Swirling green trees shaking their leaves.
Pouring rain chattering from the sky.

Matthew Brown (10)
Roe Green Junior School

I Remember, I Remember

I remember, I remember,
When I was young,
A strange dog scratched me,
Red blood poured over my leg.

I remember, I remember,
The water from the kettle,
Fell and marked.

I remember, I remember,
Being in the temple,
I was lost then my uncle found me.

I remember, I remember,
My best friend in Sri Lanka,
He was so funny.

I remember, I remember,
Having a beautiful white teddy bear,
For my birthday, saying 'Wake up.'

Sivasankar Sivakumar (9)
Roe Green Junior School

Things Come To Life

Tall, red buses roaring down the road
Shiny, green doors screeching when they open
Bright blue sky circling around the Earth
Smooth, green grass sleeping in winter until summer
Black metal gutter talking to the water as it goes down
White metal cameras spying on the children in the playground
Two tall basketball nets dancing in the playground.

Pritesh Patel (9)
Roe Green Junior School

COMING ALIVE

Glistening cars growling
Along smirking black street

Black metal cameras spying
Along the sleeping playground

Two black basketball nets
Boringly awaiting a strike

Fine sparkling trees wiggling
Under the circling sky

Two silver water fountains
Sprinkling water on the ground

The shuffling of green grass
Along the brown soil

The clear white birds
Shivering against the cold blue sky.

Mohamed Tamam (10)
Roe Green Junior School

OUR PLAYGROUND COMES ALIVE

Tall, brown trees whistling
Yellow and green cars roaring angrily
Blue and white sky circling above me
Red, round windows screeching
Long gardens sleeping
Two green doors squeaking open
Basket ball net playing
Weak green grass blowing
One tall shelter growling at me.

Priya Rabadia (9)
Roe Green Junior School

I REMEMBER, I REMEMBER

I remember, I remember
a blue and green tricycle,
very fast and very shiny.

I remember, I remember
learning to take my first steps walking
backwards and forwards.

I remember, I remember
I used to sing but I
don't write them.

I remember, I remember
when I was one-year-old,
I met my friend and his name is Sunny.
He played with me and sometimes he'd hit me.

Miten Thakrani (9)
Roe Green Junior School

THE PLAYGROUND

Fierce benches were howling,
Narrow houses whispering,
The laughing cars rustling by,
The sky circling around,
The jungle gardens chatting,
The silver cameras spying,
The deep black concrete sliding,
Yellow salt box spreading,
The see-through windows smirking,
And two basketball nets coming closer together.

Muneba Iqbal (10)
Roe Green Junior School

THINGS ALIVE

Brown wooden tree dancing
Around the playground.

Sparkling gold cars sliding
Around the street.

Grey striped cats squeaking
In the garden.

Silver edged camera spying
Around the playground.

Black gates laughing
As they open.

Two basketball nets wiggling
In the playground.

Blue steps dancing
On the spot.

Green grass chattering
In the garden.

Colourless water fountain splashing
As the water comes out.

Reema Patel (9)
Roe Green Junior School

JACKIE CHAN

Jackie Chan
He's my man,
And he can beat you up with a pan,
So beware of Chan.

Myuran Ranganathan (8)
Roe Green Junior School

I REMEMBER

I remember, I remember
My first christening and the priest pouring holy water on my head.

I remember, I remember
When I first walked, I fell down the stairs.

I remember, I remember
I was not looking and I fell down the stairs
I could not breathe and could not walk, I went to the hospital.

I remember, I remember
It was my birthday
I had my birthday party in McDonald's.

Seanie Joseph (10)
Roe Green Junior School

OUR PLAYGROUND COMES ALIVE

Two basketball nets jumping up and down
The gardens whispering along with the silver water fountains
The shiny, white window smirking
The green and brown tree dancing with the grass
The brown house chatting with the dark road
The bright, blue sky blowing the dark brown bench
The bright green door slamming the black gate
The cameras spying on the children
The concrete shaking like an earthquake
The grey step roaring at the motorcycle
The cars and the buses are shouting to the shelter.

Panitaj Bhudia (9)
Roe Green Junior School

EAST AFRICA

Lions,
    Cheetahs,
        Lion cubs hiding among the long grass,
In what used to be a pool of water that had dried up in the heat,
And made the soil crack.

Giraffes,
    Baboons,
        The thudding of elephants
Near the raging waterfalls so fierce you could see
The spray coming up in puffs of white.

Zebras,
    Hippos,
        Fierce hyena cubs,
Sleeping lazily under shady trees,
Curled up together keeping snug.

Crocodiles,
    Snakes,
        Gazelles - Thompsons and Grants, grazing on the open plains,
Twitching with every sudden movement,
Standing up tall and straight, alert to predators.

Rozina Sabur (10)
Roe Green Junior School

THE BIG YELLOW SUN

When you are out in the sun
In the nice fresh air eating a bun.
In the big yellow sun having lots of fun,
In the sun it is so much fun.

Shakti Shah (8)
Roe Green Junior School

BRING THINGS ALIVE

The black, shiny cameras spying closely
The windows sparkling and peeping
The green grass blowing and rustling
The brown gardens sleeping and roaring away
Brown gates rustling open
Grey steps wiggle and growl
The water fountain whispering and laughing
The cars beep and shine just like a star in the sky
The green trees creak and howl.

Komal Patel (9)
Roe Green Junior School

THE WEIRDEST SCHOOL ON EARTH

Square, clear windows smirking down at me.
Creepy basketball nets moving towards me.
Smoking gates blow smoke in my face as I go past.
Whispering trees in the garden whispering at me.
Snarling motorbikes roaring up the road.
Silver, shiny water fountains going on and off as they please.
Spying cameras spying on me.
Slamming door as I walk past.

Hasani James (9)
Roe Green Junior School

FIREWORKS

Fireworks, fireworks,
So bright, no wonder you can see
Pink and white beautiful colours and shapes,
Kids say, 'Oooh, aaah' and lots of sounds
Crash and bash with a cry in the sky.

Fireworks, fireworks,
High, high away from the stars,
Lots of colours to see,
Goodbye.

Preena Popat
Roe Green Junior School

COMING ALIVE

A green spooky tree rustling,
Some sneaky cameras spying,
Skidding cars roaring,
A spooky door growling,
Spiky green grass squeaking,
A black, rusty, old gate smirking,
Red buses sliding,
The blue, glimmering sky circling,
Brown, skidding benches sprinkling,
Reflected windows howling.

Anand Joshi (10)
Roe Green Junior School

THE SUN SHINES UP, UP HIGH

The sun shines up, up high,
The flowers grow to reach the sky,
Children play on the swings when there's light
Until the sky turns from day to night,
In the dark sky the moon and stars are bright,
To light up the night.

Zahra Khan (7)
Roe Green Junior School

THE PLAYGROUND

The small little
camera peeping
on the children.

The sky
blowing the
work along.

The garden
is spreading
in the dark.

The little black
cat sleeping
in the house.

The tree is
whispering to
the mouse.

The grass is
running next
to the house.

Kiran Manji (9)
Roe Green Junior School

LOVE

Love is wonderful,
Love is kind,
Love is happy,
Love is good.

Rhys Mulikita (8)
Roe Green Junior School

ELEPHANTS

Sometimes you hear a thud
in the mud.

The elephant's trunk
smells like a skunk.

He sleeps in a heap
but it's very deep.

He lives in a jungle
where there's a rumble.

The hunter is here,
but he has a fear.

Shazia Kassam (7)
Roe Green Junior School

THE GINGER CAT

Pat the cat the ginger cat
Flew down the street on a flying mat
She fell in the bin with a rat-a-tat-tat

Hey I'm Pat the cat, so sit on the mat,
I'll give you a fat scratched yummy rat
If you're my fan then join my band
Or sit there playing with the sand.

Remember when you need fun just
Shout the ginger cat - Superscratch!

Bunsri Bhuwa (9)
Roe Green Junior School

My Balloon

Up, up and away
On a beautiful sunny day.
My balloon went up the trees,
I felt a breeze.
In the fine air
I saw the birds stare.
I went past the sea
And that's where I want to be.
Now I want my balloon
To come down soon.

Shireen Mohammad (8)
Roe Green Junior School

My Name Is Jahni

My name is Jahni, I like going to school,
Sometimes I'm excited, sometimes I'm cool.
When I grow up, I want to be an aeroplane pilot,
But for that I have to go to pilot school
And learn the golden rules.

Jahni Thomas (7)
Roe Green Junior School

Winter, Winter

Winter, winter, freezing like snow,
I hope my fingers don't glow.
That's why we walk so slow,
Especially on snow.

Nidhi Shah (8)
Roe Green Junior School

COMING ALIVE

Sprinkling fountain whispering quietly.
Pouring rain chattering down from the sky.
Circling blue sky spinning around in the air.
Thundering lightning soaring through the sky.
Swirling, green tree shaking everywhere.
Screeching red bus roaring down the road.
White paper plane shooting through the silent wind.
Turning door squeaking while it turns.
Boiling hot air balloon flying through the whistling wind.

Sandeep Bharj (10)
Roe Green Junior School

THINGS COMING ALIVE

Two basketball nets creeping towards the school.
Tiny cameras spying at people walking by the garden.
Five big houses talking to each other.
A shelter whispering to the wind.
Bare trees rustling their branches.
Metal dustbins creaking at the school.
The swishing of the water fountain can be heard miles away.

Ramindra Pal M Darma Pal (9)
Roe Green Junior School

SPRING

Spring is a season when flowers grow,
Lovely green leaves grow on the trees.

People are happy for the sun is shining,
I like spring because everybody's happy.

Melissa Calleja (7)
Roe Green Junior School